WIVES ON A MISSION

TO ENDURE

STRATEGIES TO PRESS ON IN YOUR MARRIAGE WHEN YOU REALLY WANT TO QUIT

KATHERINE BROOKINS

DEDICATION

This book is dedicated to wives all over the world who feel like they are alone, stuck, miserable, and misunderstood in their marriage. Wives who sometimes feel like they made a mistake getting married, or they married the wrong person. I pray that you will read this book and realize that you are not alone in what you are going through, and you are right where God wants you to be in order for His purpose to be fulfilled and His Glory to be revealed in and through you. God sees your every effort. Continue to allow God to work on you, your husband, and your marriage and watch Him work a miracle. Keep reading, and I'll meet you in the chapters.

Table of Contents

INTRODUCTION

Hey ladies, listen up! Let me be honest. Marriage is hard. My grandma once told me it's only hard because I make it hard. But the truth is . . . even when I'm not trying to make it hard, it's hard. Even on the days that I think I'm doing what I'm supposed to do as a *good* wife, it's still complicated. There are days when I give my hubby love, respect, and words of affirmation, but it still doesn't seem to be enough. I may put my guard down and leave my heart open, but somehow my emotions still seem to get bruised. Heck, I may even give him what he wants in the bedroom as often as he wants, and sometimes I still don't see a change in our behavior towards one another. Honestly, I just don't know sometimes if we're going to make it. Divorce has called my name so many times, and for the past twelve years, I've been ignoring the call. Some days the temptation to leave this marriage is so real that I can taste freedom on the other side. Now don't get me wrong; I love the whole idea of marriage. Just being with only one person for the rest of my life is beautifully amazing. I love cuddling and just chilling at home, sometimes just doing nothing but gazing into each other's eyes and smiling. I love being one with my husband and having a forever date. I love raising our children in a two-parent household. I love it all! But sometimes the constant arguments over the little things make me wonder if being married is worth the headache. I'm talking about things so little that in the middle of the argument you both forget what you were arguing about. To avoid looking crazy, one of you just pulls something out of the hat from the past to prove your point because you forgot how the argument started in the first place, which means you really don't have a point. Yeah, those crazy little arguments that have you not talking to each other for days. Yet, you both are too petty, immature, and prideful to be the first one to apologize. Yeah, those arguments.

Before you get to thinking *her marriage must be horrible*, let me just say it, "No, I don't have a horrible marriage." I do not have a bad marriage at all. Bad moments, yes, but not an overall bad marriage, and to be honest I had to learn that. I used to think my marriage, heck my life, was horrible . . . until I changed my perspective. God has opened my eyes, and I now see the beauty in my life and my marriage. My marriage is pretty good actually. It's a regular marriage with regular problems. I thank God that cheating is not our issue, and we're both honest about our feelings. But baby let me tell you, it's the constant bickering and arguing over nothing that's weighing me down. I guess that's why there is an option to get a divorce over irreconcilable differences, which is the audacity to go to court and say we don't have any real issues, we just can't get along. "But why?" the Judge might ask. Imagine a wife saying to the judge, "Because I no longer like the way he chews gum or squeezes the toothpaste, and I don't feel loved by him anymore. He just doesn't support me the way that I would like him to. I thought I could deal with it for a lifetime but after ten years, I can't stand it anymore." The Judge might ask the husband, "Sir why do you want to divorce your wife?" Imagine a husband saying, "Well your honor, she's a beautiful woman inside and out but she's just not as domesticated as I would like for her to be. I understand she's trying to build a career and raise the kids, but I want a woman who'll cook and clean for me all the time. I want to wake up to breakfast in bed with my house shoes waiting by the bed for me. I want a woman who doesn't mind making home-cooked meals for me every day on top of making sure the kids are taken care of. I want a woman who serves me and respects me as a man and as her husband. My wife cooks sometimes, but she's always saying she's tired or has some other excuse. She also makes the kids clean up behind themselves, and they don't do it right, so I want her to do it. Yet, she won't do it because she keeps saying she's trying to teach them how to take care of themselves when they leave the house, but I want my house cleaned right now! Since she won't do it when I ask, I want a divorce." I can only imagine how the judge would look at a couple like this sideways for wasting his or her precious time, especially when he or she probably has other divorce cases to tend to that may have real, severe trauma and problems.

I'm a Godly Christian woman, and the fear of the Lord keeps me from getting a divorce. My husband and I have been together for more than a decade. Our long union is not because we have been such awesome spouses to one another, but because of our reverential fear and respect for God and his word concerning marriage and divorce. I believe if I wasn't a believer, I would have quit a long time ago. However, because I love the Lord, my husband, my children, and the idea of my future legacy, I fight for my marriage. Not physically, but spiritually. And, so does my husband. Heck, even our children pray for our marriage sometimes, when both my husband and I are too done with each other to pray. For this reason, it's good to teach your children how and when to pray. I often tell myself I don't want to be disobedient and disappoint God. However, I also don't want to be married for years and be miserable.

Neither do I want to be divorced. I often feel like I'm in a battle that's in its own category. Someone once told me, "Kat, it seems like you've only given yourself two options: be married and miserable or get a divorce. Being happily married for a lifetime isn't even one of your options." I had to think about that thing for a minute and let it settle in. Like *Lord, what battle am I really fighting here? Am I fighting the stigma of divorce in my family? Or, am I fighting to stay married and happy?* All I heard was . . . *both.* And, it just came over me that not only do I have to fight the temptation of getting a divorce, but I also have to learn how to be in a healthy God-fearing marriage full of happiness, love, respect, peace, service, and joy. I say *learn* because no one taught me how to be a good wife, and no one taught me how to be in a healthy relationship, let alone a healthy marriage. I had to ask God, "How do I maintain a healthy and loving marriage? Because I'm getting my butt kicked over here by the devil in spiritual warfare. Besides Lord, I've never seen that type of marriage up close. How do I become something I've never seen before? Or live a life that I never saw? And how do I stay in the fight when I'm weary and I want to give up?" Well, ladies here we go! I've been married for nearly thirteen years, and I pray that the Lord will give me the strength, love, patience, endurance, respect, and honor I need for my husband and vice versa so that we can make it through a lifetime in a beautiful, healthy marriage. We want a marriage designed by God that can be an example to all. In this book, I'll share with you the tips and strategies that God has given me to make it this far. I pray that it blesses you and your marriage as it has helped me. As I pray for your marriage to endure and last, please pray for longevity and godly joy over my marriage as well.

I am a Wife on a Mission to Endure. I don't mean to endure in terms of suffering; God doesn't want that for us. I mean to endure in terms of lasting a lifetime. With that being said, *Wives on a Mission to Endure* is a mission created to help wives endure the challenges of marriage in order to learn, grow, and enjoy the fruit of their labor with their husbands. We use biblical principles to help you transform your mindset about you, your husband, and your marriage as well as help you go from thinking about divorce to thinking about life more abundantly with the husband you have now. I pray that this book is a blessing to you, your husband, and your marriage. I wrote the book in hopes of ministering to myself and being a support to other wives. You may feel overwhelmed in your marriage and the only easy way out of the unhappiness you see is divorce. Yet, deep down inside you don't want a divorce, you want to do the necessary changes within to make your marriage survive and thrive, but you don't know how. Well, this book is for you! Again, I've been married for nearly thirteen years. To the more seasoned wives, that's not long at all, but I believe you can still get something out of this book, or you can probably relate to it. For some wives, they can't even imagine themselves making it as far as I have. I am no expert by a long shot, and I regularly pray that God will bless my marriage so that it can be a blessing. There are some days that I am very confident that my husband and I will remain married for a lifetime, grow old together, and live to see our great-great-grandchildren. Then there are some days that I just don't know if we have the strength to make it another year. These are the days that I lean more on God's strength rather than my own, for God's strength is made perfect in my weakness. The information I give is from my own experience. No one but the Holy Spirit taught me how to be a wife, as I never saw a healthy marriage growing up. And, the same goes for my husband. No one but the Holy Spirit taught him how to be a husband. And like me, he didn't see a healthy marriage growing up. We both came to the marriage ignorant to the significance of the covenant and blinded by a cute face and a ring. The lessons that I learned in this book are straight from the Holy Spirit. These are the tools God gave me when I felt like I was at my wit's end and didn't think I could make it through another year of marriage. You and I are on this journey of having an everlasting marriage together. Pray for mine as I pray for yours. Again, I'm not an expert, but dive into these chapters and get the lessons that the expert himself, the Holy Spirit, gave to me to endure the test of time. Now let's dive in!

And the Lord answered me, and said, Write the vision, and make it plain upon tables, that he may run that readeth it (Habakkuk 2:2, KJV).

My sister-in-law and I had begun talking to each other every Saturday. We came together to pray for our marriage and encourage each other not to give up the good fight of marriage. After one of my venting sessions with her, I poured out my heart saying, "I've been doing this for eleven years. I will not go another eleven years of marriage if it is going to be like this." I believe she was surprised to hear these words come out of my mouth. She was a newlywed and for the last few weeks leading up to this conversation, I had been the one encouraging her, and now the shoe was on the other foot, and I was the one who needed to be encouraged. I told her I'm going to give this marriage two more years because I'll be forty by then. I didn't want to waste all of my youthful years on a marriage that was barely making it.

I said, "If it's still in this condition in two years, then I'm quitting."

She then said, "You know what, let's pray because you're not done. God wants to use you and your Husband in a mighty way. We're going to celebrate y'all 50th wedding anniversary, and you're going to help plenty of wives. So, let's just get rid of that thought now. We're going to look back in two years when you're still married and laugh at this moment."

I said, "If you say so," and chuckled. As she began to pray for me, I heard the Lord say "Wives on a Mission to Endure" so clearly. Then, I saw a glimpse of a conference for wives who were ready to throw in the towel and give up on their marriage. When she finished praying, I told her what I had heard and seen.

I said, "Let's do a conference for wives and give them what we have here with each other, prayer and encouragement."

She said, "Aw, ok."

I don't think she really took me seriously at that moment, but little did she know, a light bulb had lit up in my mind, and it would not shut off. Every day, I was texting her new ideas that were coming to my mind. She too began to get excited as she realized that I wasn't joking; I was for real. She started texting me ideas. This went on for weeks until we finally said, "Ok, now let's put our ideas into action." Thus, we created our first conference, *Wives on a Mission to Endure,* on May 22, 2021. It was a great success!

I created the conference and wrote this book because, in the marriages that surrounded me that ended in divorce, I noticed that it was the wife who quit. The wife gave up and took action to get the divorce. I thought, *Lord, what is going on? Why are these wives quitting? What's the final straw that's making these wives give up on their marriage?*

CHAPTER 2: MARRIAGE IS AN ASSIGNMENT

And they shall be one flesh . . . And God blessed them, and God said unto them, Be fruitful, and multiply, and replenish the earth, and subdue it . . . (Genesis 2:24, 1:28, KJV).

"It is not good for man to be alone, I will make him a helpmeet . . . and the two shall be one flesh" (Genesis 2:18, KJV). When God created the woman for the man, he had the man's needs in mind, not his desires. For God fulfilled a need that Adam didn't even know that he had. In the same way, God gives us our husbands to fulfill needs that we sometimes don't even know that we have. Sometimes those needs are revealed immediately, and sometimes they are not revealed until later times in our marital lives, from the smallest to greatest of our needs. For example, I am 4'11, and I'm a very petite woman. My husband is about 6'5 and about 245 pounds. The man is built like a black stallion—just tall, dark, and oh so handsome. When we first started dating, I had an apartment with a washer and dryer in it. So, any time I needed to wash, I would just take my clothes to my laundry room and wash them with no hassle. When we got married, we moved out of state, and our new apartment did not have a washer and dryer in the unit. Due to this, we had to go to the laundromat to wash our clothes. You can only imagine how many bags of clothes a family of eight can make in a week or two. We would sort and pack the clothes together, but my husband had to be the one to carry those heavy bags up and down the stairs, to and from our car, and in and out of the laundromat. Even when going grocery shopping, I have to ask him to get items off the top shelf for me. If my husband is not around, and I just absolutely cannot reach something, I sometimes have to walk around and find someone tall enough to get it for me. Yes, I'm that short. My husband is big, strong, and tall, so he gets the heavy and high stuff. In hindsight, God knew that my little self would need a tall strong husband to get by easier in this world. I say easier because we women will scream independent all day, especially if we grew up in a family of independent women who *doesn't need a man*. As women, we know how to get by and figure things out. I'm sure if I was a single mom like I was when my husband and I first met, I would have figured the whole laundry bag situation out so that I can wash my family's clothes, but that's not my point. My point is that I didn't have to figure it out. Because before I knew what I needed, from the most important thing to the least important, God knew. And he provided my needs, and some of my wants, in my husband and vice-a-versa. God knew that although I'm small in stature, I'm tall when it comes to strength, courage, wisdom, faith, boldness, and tenacity. Likewise, my husband was going to need a little firecracker like me to take bold faith moves that will cause him to increase his faith and get out of his comfort zone. My husband and I are both believers in Jesus Christ and our spiritual gifts complement each other. Where I'm weak, he is strong, and where he is weak, I'm strong. God designed us this way. Although we are two separate individuals who can operate on our own, we're better together operating as one. I am bone of his bones and flesh of his flesh (Genesis 2:23, KJV). He and I are whole when we stand alone, but we are a dynamic duo and a double threat to the kingdom of darkness when we stand together. For this, I say that I am my husband's assignment, and he is mine. I cannot fail; I will not fail. God gave me this assignment because he felt that I could handle it. Who am I to say that the Lord was wrong by abandoning the mission he gave me. Think about school. When our teachers give us an assignment, it's up to us to study the material so when test day comes, we will pass. Some of us get the syllabus at the beginning of the semester that lists the reading material, all the upcoming assignments, and their due dates, as well as future quizzes and test dates. Yet, we still fail the course and will even blame it on the teacher and say that they graded our assignments harshly. We might also say that our teachers didn't let us slide on some assignments that we thought we should have slid on. The truth is you cannot blame anyone but yourself. You received a heads up in the syllabus and you knew what you were supposed to do. However, you didn't care enough or put forth enough effort to read the book and study. Some of us fail because we think we know more than the teacher. We take some of the easier courses for granted and slack off. Therefore, we end up failing the easier course all because we thought that it was so easy that we didn't have to put in the work. This is due to us thinking we know the material already. However, when test day came and it asked you questions that were only from the course textbook and not from basic knowledge, you failed. You failed a simple easy-going class because you didn't make the course your priority. You wouldn't humble yourself and take the time out to read the book. You wasted time, money, and energy, and now you have to retake the course. This is how the assignment of marriage is. It seems simple. Man finds a wife, finds a good thing, and obtains favor from the Lord (Proverbs 18:22, KJV). Well, this makes it sound simple like no work needs to be done. We have this *Well, God brought us together and he's going to keep us together* mentality. Yes, that's true on some level, but you still have to do your homework. You have to study your husband. What does he like or dislike? What's his love language (Read Gary Chapman's *The Five Love Languages*)? What makes him tick? What gets him in the mood? What turns him off? What makes him laugh, cry, or smile? When is the best time to approach him or not approach him about the finances? Does he like to relax first when he comes home from work, or does he enjoy the kids bum rushing him when he first walks through the door? Does he know how to give good gifts? Or, should you give him grace in this area because you see his efforts? My point is your husband is your assignment. Have you studied him lately? Or, have you gotten so comfortable with him that you think you know him so well that you haven't even noticed a change in him? You haven't even noticed his growth. Wives, just like us, our husbands are forever evolving, forever changing. What worked five years ago, might not work today. Sure, he is the same man you married genetically, but if you open your eyes and pay more attention to his growth, and not just your own, you will notice that mentally, physically, spiritually, and emotionally he has changed. He doesn't even hold you the same way he used to. Instead of taking it personally by giving him the silent treatment or assuming that he's cheating, have you asked him why? Maybe it has nothing to do with you. Maybe he's gained weight, and he feels that you're so beautiful that you can't possibly still be attracted to him. Remember this, he is your man! No one else but yours. If your husband is cheating on the test by looking at someone else's paper, then tell the teacher. Simply put, if your husband is committing adultery, you as the wife have the authority to cast satan out, but not by fighting flesh with flesh. God gave you two this assignment. No one else is supposed to be involved in it. If your husband is sharing his answers with someone else, then walk up to the teacher's desk (the throne of God), get on your knees, and spill the beans. Yes, tell the teacher. Tell God. He is our teacher and our disciplinarian. He is our principal in this whole school of marriage and this school of life. You cannot get your husband straight. No amount of nagging, back and forth arguments, threats to leave if he doesn't get his act together, or *I'm going to get him back* stunts are going to change whatever situation you and your husband are in. If you want to win, then you have to become totally sold out and surrendered to Jesus. It's the only way. I can't give you anything else but Jesus. He transformed my mind. Once I started looking at my marriage, my husband, and my children as assignments from God, it changed the whole trajectory of my life. Now if something is off, I think, *What lesson is this? What season are we in? It's time for me to study and do my research again; something has changed. I missed something. What book in the Bible do I need to study for this season? When was the last time I studied my husband?* Sis, if you don't study your husband, there's some chick somewhere waiting for you to fall, so she can. I used to hate when people would tell me that, but it is so true. I've seen it with my own eyes. There would be women who wouldn't say two words to me, maybe a hello and a goodbye, but they would get around my husband and tell him their whole life story. I am like, *Now wait a doggone minute. Why is she telling you all her business like that?* I'll always tell my husband that if a woman has a question about marriage, she needs to be talking to me or talking to both of us together. Now, we have some female friends that we just love wholeheartedly, and they love us as a couple and are not out to harm us. I don't mind my husband talking to them because they don't care if they talk to me or him, as long as they get God in the situation that they are going through. If they talk to him, they would sometimes tell him they prefer to speak to me, and we would laugh as I picked up the phone. Sometimes I would tell them to talk to my husband because they need a man's opinion on the matter. I am not a jealous woman. I am, however, a wife with spiritual discernment. I am not going to walk behind my husband trying to micro-manage every conversation he has with someone of the opposite sex. That's where trust and love come in. I have to trust that he loves me enough to be able to govern himself as a God-fearing husband when he is having conversations with other women, especially when I'm not around. He expects the same from me. We are both human beings, and we will have to encounter people of the opposite sex on our jobs, at church, and at the stores. I refuse to be on my husband's hip with every move he makes because I think another woman is going to take him. Absolutely not, no ma'am. I have too much to do with my own life to be hounding that man like that. It's draining and stressful if I have to check his phone every time he comes home, ask him what women he talked to today, check his pockets, and so on. No, Ma'am. Ain't nobody got time for that! Not this one. As I stated before, I am a discerning wife. So, if I sense that a woman is up to no good, I will warn him to be careful in his conversations with certain people. I find the following behaviors to be considered red flags:

1. A woman who walks right past you and does not speak or her conversation is short with

you, but then she gets to your husband and speaks or all of a sudden, she becomes Chatty Patty when she talks to him.

2. A woman who asks him things that she could've asked you, like *Oh, how are your kids doing?* You're thinking, *Didn't you just see me with my kids? Why didn't you ask me?*

3. Women who make unnecessary small talk with your husband just to be near him and have a conversation.

4. Any woman who is *extra* friendly with you when your husband is around is questionable. You would think, *Girl you just saw me in the bathroom and didn't even look up to smile at me. Now I come out and my husband introduces you to me and you smile from ear to ear* saying, "Aw, this is your wife? I just saw her in the bathroom. It's so nice to meet you. I like your dress." You think to yourself, *Girl bye! You could have told me that in the lady's room. Stop making stuff up to be seen. You didn't know I was his wife. You got caught up and now you looking stupid to me trying to front and make up for it. Woman to woman we both know what you're doing so cut the nonsense. You just became a red flag.*

As always, I give my hubby the watch her speech, and in my quiet time with God, I cover him in prayer. Or, even I'll pray over him in our prayer time together. We are to watch and pray. Not hound and nag. There have been times where he would be naive, disagree, and say, "Baby that person is just being nice."

I would say, "Yeah ok, whatever."

I don't go back and forth. I go to daddy God and pray, *Lord if I'm wrong about this person, forgive me and fix my heart*

20

and emotions concerning this individual. Lord, if I'm not wrong and there is some ill-intent on this person's part or if they have some ulterior motive, open my husband's eyes so that he may see the truth. Then days, weeks, or months later, he would come back and say that he noticed that she walked right past me and didn't speak, and then came right to him and held a conversation like she didn't just ignore me. Then he would apologize, promise to keep his distance, and be mindful of his interactions with that person. We pretty much have a mutual agreement when it comes to how each other deals with the opposite sex. We trust each other in that area, and that's the way a healthy marriage should be.

The trust should be so strong in your marriage that you and your spouse could switch phones if need be. For example, if my phone is dead, I leave mine at home on the charger and ask my husband for his, walk out the door, and run my errands with no problem. Now granted I would rather have my phone because I'm used to it, and it has all of my apps. The point of the matter is we are not trying to hide anything from each other, and that's just the kind of trust that we have built for each other in that specific area.

I said all that to say that your marriage is your assignment. You are to cover it in prayer. You are to stay on the wall and pray until God answers. You are to intercede and stand in the gap on behalf of your husband and children. You are to war for your marriage when the time comes. The bible says what God has joined together, let no man put asunder (Matthew 19:6, KJV). So, no one can come along and just take what God has given you. If the marriage is falling or has fallen apart, that is because one or both of you have relinquished your rights and left an open door for Satan to creep in. If you are both emotionally and spiritually fighting and standing in the gap for your marriage, you leave no room for the enemy. Therefore, God has to come to your rescue. If you both have decided to allow God to be the center in your marriage, then as long as you continue to walk the path he has set before you, the two of you will be okay. That doesn't mean your life and marriage will be problem-free. It just means that "No weapon that is formed against thee shall prosper" (Isaiah 54:17, KJV).

In addition, marriage is an assignment from God, but like my grandma once told me, marriage is what you make it. If you have decided in your mind that you are going to have a miserable marriage, then that is what you will have. People can try to convince you otherwise, but until you get that, you will not see the beauty in your own marriage. You will only see your marital flaws. Change your perspective, you change your vision, your life, and your marriage for the better.

CHAPTER 3: THE BLESSINGS AND PROMISES OF GOD

For all of God's promises have been fulfilled in Christ with a resounding "Yes!" And through Christ, our "Amen" (which means "Yes") ascends to God for his glory (2 Corinthians 1:20, NLT).

In the previous chapter, we talked about the assignment of marriage. In this chapter, I want to expound on the fact that when you leave your assignment prematurely, by way of a divorce, you miss out on the promises of God that are attached to your marriage. There are some blessings that God has set aside strictly for you and your husband to obtain. I remember when we first got married. The thought of divorce and separation plagued my mind so heavily, and God told me, *Sure you can get a divorce. I still will be with you, but you will miss out on some of the many blessings that I have for you that are attached to this marriage. You will not reach your fullest potential in Me that can only come from you staying in this marriage.* I didn't understand or even know the value of those blessings and promises then, but I do know now.

About the second year into our marriage, the Lord told my husband and me that we will have a son together. He gave me the middle name for our son. Then later He gave my husband the first name. This was so exciting to us because we are a blended family, and by this time, we had four children in all. I had one son when we met, and my husband had two kids, both a daughter and a son. Together we had one daughter. So, we already had a daughter together, and now wanted a son too. Biologically, I had two kids at the time, one boy and one girl. I had always shared with God, even before I met my husband, that I wanted two girls and two boys. I didn't know if He would give them to me like that, but that did not stop me from asking. The Bible says ask and ye shall receive (Matthew 7:7-8, KJV). Well, I asked and was waiting to receive it. Yep, I put my order in with the Lord, as if I was ordering at a restaurant, asking God for the number of girls and boys that I wanted. Anyway, about four years into our marriage I got pregnant again with what would be our first child together born under a covenant. All our other children had been born prior to us being married. We were super excited about this pregnancy because it was intentional, and this time we were actually trying to get pregnant because God had made us a promise, years before, that we would have a son together. Because of our planning, we already had a name for our unborn son. We were ready to go through this pregnancy with great joy and anticipation. We started going through prenatal care. We would rub my belly and call our son's name with every movement in my belly. We would smile and say we're finally having a son together. We went to our ultrasound visit to reveal the gender of our baby, and they revealed to us that we were having another girl.

> *What? That can't be right. Those technicians don't know what they're talking about. This is a boy because the Lord told us we are going to have a son together, and this is our son that we are having to-ge-ther! Besides, I already have two children, and I knew what their gender was going to be before I had them because I could feel it.*

I gave birth to my other two children in another state and assumed the technicians in my current state of residence didn't know their stuff. I thought to myself, *How are they going to tell me what I'm having? I know my body, and I got it right the last two times. Maybe we should give it some*

24

more time. It's probably still too early for them to know for sure.
So, we went to our next ultrasound, and sure enough, they said, "It's a girl!" Oh, well my husband and I were not hearing that. We were just not in agreement with the technicians. I truly thought that something must be wrong with the machine because, by this time, I'm about six months pregnant which means they could clearly see the gender of the baby. However, we didn't believe the doctors because the LORD told us we were going to have a son. We heard God so who is man to say otherwise. It's funny now, but back then we were in such disbelief that this wasn't our promised son. When people would ask us what we were having, we would tell them that we thought we were having a boy. They would look at how far along I was and ask what the doctors said. We would tell them that the doctors believe it's a girl, but that's not what the Lord told us so we're going with a boy. People would look at us like we were crazy, young, foolish, and immature, but we didn't think so. We were both on one accord. People would tell us to believe the ultrasound, and I would sigh in disagreement and inform them that I wasn't wrong with predicting the gender of my other two children. Well, we went to our final ultrasound, and our ultrasound technician looked and said, "Oh yes, you're having a girl for sure, look at the screen." We looked and couldn't deny it ourselves. Our daughter had her legs wide open in my womb, and you can clearly see that she was a girl. It was as if she was saying, *I had enough with y'all saying that I'm a boy. I AM A GIRL!* The technician was able to take the picture and give it to us for our memory. We laugh every time we tell that story, especially to our daughter. She was bold then, and she is a little bold firecracker for the Lord now. We couldn't imagine life without her. However, at the time

of my pregnancy, my husband and I were very disappointed. We questioned if we even heard God at all. Surely, family and friends laughed at us saying, "I told you so." We were humiliated! We prayed, *Lord, we trusted you! We made a fool of ourselves having faith in the promise that we thought we heard you tell us.* At this point, I'm about eight months pregnant, and we did not have a name. We were so big on thinking we had a boy that we didn't think of any girl's name at all. Not one name came to mind, not one.

I went to work later that week, and I worked in the admissions office in higher education. I had to manually add all the incoming applications into the school's database. I had a list of about 150 names, both boys and girls. So, I had the idea to look at this list for a nice girl name.

I would call my husband, and ask, "What about this name?"

"No," he would say, "I don't like that."

"Ok, what about this?"

"No, too plain."

"This?"

"Too old."

"And this?"

"Absolutely not!"

Finally, after going almost through the whole list, I said, "What about Olivia?"

He said, "Ah, that's perfect! It's like the olive that they use to make olive oil to anoint God's people. We thought about whether we knew any Olivia's that were corrupt, and we couldn't think of anybody. All the Olivia's we knew, which were a few, had such sweet personalities. So, we settled on Olivia, and she is every bit of her name bold, beautiful and strong. We didn't have our promised son yet, but we saw the blessing in having Olivia.

For the Lord God is our sun and our shield. He gives us grace and glory. The Lord will withhold no good thing from those who do what is right (Psalm 84:11, NLT).

Two years had passed since Olivia was born. We had been trying again with hopes of getting pregnant, but nothing happened until two years later. Again, like the last pregnancy, we were super excited. *Could this be our boy, or could the combination of our genes only make girls?* Knowing that God told us that we would have a son together, but afraid of what happened in the last pregnancy, we decided not to know the gender of the baby until we gave birth. We went old school. This was the most exciting and nervous pregnancy I had ever had. First, I knew this would be my absolute last pregnancy because I was considered high risk. This would be my fourth time giving birth, which would mean my fourth cesarean section, better known as a C-Section. Due to the high risk, my doctor monitored me very closely, and I had more prenatal visits than normal just to check the health of the baby.

I'm a petite woman, and with my first child, my doctor said at the rate that my child was growing, and with my small frame, it probably would be best if I just go straight into getting a C-section. I told him no because I wanted to at least try to go into labor on my own. I had seen the women on TV pushing, screaming, and cursing out the father of their child saying, "Why did you do this to meeeeeee!?" I too wanted to be that dramatic. I wasn't saved then, and God had not yet cleansed my tongue. So, yes cursing during labor was at the top of my list. I wanted to hear them say, "PUSH!" I would push, only to have to repeat the process over and over again with sweat dripping from my forehead and my hair all sweated out like the women in the movies, but noooooo, that didn't happen for me. About four to five hours into my labor, my doctor said he was just going to move forward with the C-section. He said something about the umbilical cord, and he may have said something about it being wrapped around a part of my baby's body. It's been so long I can't remember. My oldest is now fourteen. The doctor also said he didn't want to put the baby under so much stress, and that judging by the size of the baby and my petite frame, he didn't want the baby to break my pelvic bone if I recall correctly. I remember thinking, *But wait, I didn't get a chance to push and cuss.* I was so disappointed that I couldn't experience natural birth because I remember them telling me that once I have a C-section, all of my births will have to be via C-section. I remember being upset with the doctor and the hold process. Looking back, I don't think he gave me enough time to even be in labor. I hear about women who were in labor for hours and days and *bloop,* the baby pops out. I remember thinking I can never tell my child I was in labor with him for twenty-two hours 59 minutes and 22.7 seconds, or whatever odd numbers mothers tell their children who get to acting up. I thought to myself about my doctor, *He just wanted to give me a C-section anyway because I hear they get paid more for C-sections.* I was angry, disappointed, and scared all at the same time. I had never been cut before. I remember calling my mother who was in another state and telling her that I was afraid to get cut. I had never had surgery before.

"I'm scared, Momma!" I stated.

29

"It's okay, baby. You're going to be okay. Mommy had you and your brothers by C-Section. You're going to do just fine," my mom comforted me. After the pep talk over the phone from my mom, I told my doctor that I was ready to prepare for the C-section, and they quickly got me prepared. My 4'11 body gave birth to a nine pounds five ounces 21 inches long baby boy.

I had another child about two years later, by my then-boyfriend, who's now my husband, and, this time it was a girl. My dynamic duo. I had the best of both worlds, one boy and one girl. Because of the closeness of the pregnancy, she was also born via a C-section. She was a little plump baby, too, and was just as bright and pink as she could be. My husband didn't share this with me until a while later, but when he saw her being delivered he was wondering whose little chubby pink baby is that. His two other children, not by me, had both been born prematurely and could almost fit in the palm of his hands. Our daughter was the first full-term baby he had at the time, and he was used to seeing tiny babies. To him small sized babies were normal, but to me, big babies were normal because that's what I kept having. So, when our daughter came out eight pounds five ounces, he said he second-guessed if he was the father. We laugh at that now because she looks and acts just like him.

Our first and second daughters, that we had together, were born about five years apart; they are my second and third children. So, I tried to do a VBAC (Vaginal Birth After Cesarean). I was determined to push a baby out. I had searched for a doctor who specializes in VBAC, and when I found one, I was confident that he could deliver my baby vaginally. However, on the day of delivery for my third child, which was our second daughter together, my labor and delivery staff opted out saying that I had not dilated in the hours of me being there, and they didn't want to risk my uterus rupturing. Again, I was disappointed. This was my last and final chance to have a vaginal birth, but it just didn't work out for me. However, God knew best. I went in to have my third C-section, which caused my doctors to recommend that I don't have any more babies because each C-section had weakened my uterus. Therefore, when I got pregnant after this, and for the fourth time, the doctors labeled me as high risk and urged me not to get pregnant again because with each pregnancy my risk level heightens. We decided to follow the doctor's orders, and we decided that this fourth pregnancy would be the last.

With that being said, we prayed:

Lord, you promised us that we will have a son together, and you even gave us his name. We know we heard you and we know your promises are true. The doctor said that this should be the last go-round. We know that you have given them wisdom, but we also know that you have the final say. If it be your will, let the baby in my womb be our promised son, in Jesus's name Amen.

We left it at that. Having faith, but at the same time learning our lesson from the last time, we moved through this pregnancy differently. Since I knew that this would be my last pregnancy, I decided to take advantage of the things I didn't do in my first pregnancy, such as Lamaze class. In addition to the Lamaze Class, we took pregnancy photos, got a 3D Ultrasound (we received pictures from the baby's chest up), and my husband and I did an at-home belly cast. I did two just in case. We just had a ball with this pregnancy. We figured if we were leaving the pregnancy game forever, then we might as well go out with a bang. We also didn't want to know the gender of our baby because we were too nervous and scared that we would be wrong again. What if we didn't hear God tell us we would have a son together, and we were going off our own assumptions of what we wanted? The last pregnancy brought about shame and embarrassment and an open door to ridicule. Not the pregnancy itself, that was beautiful. It was our boldness, and how wrong we were that was a little embarrassing. At every ultrasound check, we would tell the tech that we didn't want to know the gender of our baby to prevent them from blurting it out. For this reason, although they took full-body pictures of the baby for themselves, they only gave us ultrasound pictures from the waist up. It was fun for us as well as my extended family. My mother, brother, cousins, aunts, uncle, grandma were all in on it.

"It's a boy look at the hands," some would say.

"No, look at the nose, it's another girl," others would say.
In my mind I would say, *Not another girl, I have two already. Lord, please let this be the boy you promised.* I know some pregnant people say they just want a healthy baby. Sometimes I think they are not being honest with their true feelings and don't want to say what gender they want for fear that they won't get it.

So fast forward to delivery day. They were prepping me to get me prepared for my fourth and final C-section. It was final, not just because the doctors recommended it to me, but also because I believe as a woman, you know when you're done having kids. Of course, God has the last say so, but you can tell when your baby-making days are over. For me, after I had my third child, I would see pregnant women and think *Oh, I want to be pregnant again. I want to feel a little bundle of joy moving in my belly.* Then I would see a newborn baby and think, *Oh, baby, I want another one.* This let me know that I still had one more in me. However, after my last pregnancy, I would see a pregnant woman and think, *Ooowww, better her than me.* Sometimes, I would see a newborn baby, smile, and keep it moving honey. No, sir. No, Ma'am. It won't happen to me again unless the Lord works a miracle, okay! Anyway, they were prepping me, and they had to give me an injection in my back to numb my legs. For some reason, I was more nervous and scared about it than I had ever been before. The nursing staff was telling me to curl my back like a cat, which I knew to do, but the anticipation of that long needle and cold medicine going through my spine was making me jerk. Even as I'm writing about it, I'm cringing. Although it was nearly six years ago, I sometimes relive that moment and can still feel that needle going in my back just as the day it happened, which is crazy. I have gone through it four times, but I don't really remember the other three times. However, that last time stood out to me. That's how I knew I was done. It wasn't the labor that made me realize that I was done having kids because I was numb and couldn't feel anything. It wasn't the pregnancy because I think pregnancy itself is a beautiful experience. It was that doggone shot that had me saying to my husband, "I don't want to do this anymore, baby. I just don't want to go through this again. This is it for me." He wiped my tears and ensured me that I didn't have to go through it again. Husbands, they have it easy. They just have to watch from the sideline and be an excellent coach. We on the other hand, due to Eve's disobedience, have to endure the pain of labor—in whatever form, natural or C-section. Our bodies go through dramatic changes and have to get poked and primed for every pregnancy. Yet, on the flip side, along with not being able to experience the pain of labor, they do not get an opportunity to experience the beauty of pregnancy. To be able to watch your belly grow from month to month or to be able to feel and see your baby kick and move around in your belly. To be able to carry and birth life is such a beautiful thing.

My husband wasn't allowed to be in the room as they were administering the anesthesia. He had to wait to come in for the actual procedure. Plus, he had to get prepped with the proper garment to be in the delivery room with me. He wasn't in the room to hold my hand and give me that good forehead kiss and words of encouragement as they gave me the epidural. But God!! He always has a Ram in the bush. One nurse had just clocked in for the day, and she was just so joyful and chipper. She asked me if I wanted to hold her hand. I said, "Yes!" I didn't know this lady from a can of paint, but when I tell you I rested my head on that lady's chest, and at that moment it felt like the best place in the world to be. It felt like I was resting in the arms of the Lord. It was so soothing, so calming, so safe. It felt like God Himself had sent her there specifically for me. I began squeezing her tightly. She started rubbing my head and encouraging me. I don't know who that nurse was. I wouldn't be able to pick her out if I wanted to. I just remember her sweet touch and her calming voice. All I can do is tell the Lord thank you for sending me an angel that day. God truly looks out for his children.

So, I'm lying on the surgery table, my hubby is holding my hand. We heard the cries of a baby, and the doctor said, "It's a BOY!" My husband and I started bursting into smiles and tears. The doctor and nursing staff were all shouting with excitement. They knew our story and knew we didn't know what the gender was but were hoping for a boy with us. They, too, were super excited, and some were in tears with us. My husband and I were thanking God that He didn't let up on His promise to us. We had indeed heard that we will have a son together, and we did in God's timing. We were super excited, and my husband kept kissing me on my forehead.

He's here! I can't believe our baby boy is here. We had been waiting on him for about six years. That's how long it had been since God gave us the name and the promise of having a son together. While they were cleaning our baby up, they were completing my surgery. I had put in for a tubal ligation, so as to not risk getting pregnant again. I had put the order in with God for two girls and two boys, and he had delivered just what I wanted and then some. Thank you, Lord!! Out of protocol, the doctor asked my husband and me if we were sure we wanted to go ahead with the tubal ligation because it is a permanent procedure. My husband and I looked at each other and looked at the doctor, and together said, "Tie those tubes up!" Everybody laughed because we said it together and on one accord as if we had rehearsed and planned it that way, but we didn't. We said he's baby number six, and we do not need anymore. At this point not only did I have my now four, but we also had full custody of my husband's two children, my bonus babies, and all of them were 10 and under. So, we couldn't even conceive the thought of having another child. I told the doctor to burn them, clip them, sew them, and do whatever else he needed to do. It's a wrap for me. Again, we all laughed. It was such a joyous occasion, even the staff that we had in labor and delivery were such a blessing from beginning to end.

I started the last chapter off by saying that marriage is an assignment, and when we leave our marriage prematurely, we miss out on some of the many blessings that are attached to that assignment, which is our marriage. Ours were children and many other things that came along over the years. Yours could be something different. My point is that whatever promises and blessings that are due to that marriage begin to manifest and are poised to launch when you say, *I do.* On the contrary, it gets cut off the minute you say *I don't* want this marriage anymore, and you decide to get a divorce. Again, it took six years before God delivered on His promise.

God's promise turned out to be such an awesome little boy who at the tender age of five is on fire for the Lord, as all our children are. I'm chuckling as I type because just today, I asked him the location of a Bible scripture that I was texting to someone, and at the moment, I couldn't remember the location of that very familiar scripture. I remember it had been his homework from school, and I asked him, "Hey, where in the Bible is the scripture we all sin and fall short of the glory of God?" He yelled from the bathroom while putting up his toothbrush that it was Romans 3:23. Of course, I went to check before I texted and sent it. After all, he is five. When I went to the Bible and saw that he was correct, I couldn't stop smiling. That boy really loves the Lord and Godly things at such a young age. He came into my room, and with a smile still on my face, I thanked him for giving me the location of that scripture and told him he really helped me out. He smiled and told me that I was welcome as he walked out of the room, smiling with more confidence than he did when he came in. It was so adorable, and for me, it was a proud mommy moment. I can't imagine life without him or any of my children for that matter. To see this little being, who was once a thought, actually walking, talking, and breathing is so amazing to me. With my eyes watery, and the smile still on my face, I took a deep breath and thanked the Lord for all the things He has given me and the many things that I asked for that He didn't give me. Thank you, Father.

One of the many things that he didn't give me that I had asked for was a divorce from my husband. I'm so glad that God looked over those moments that I was in my feelings, screaming, praying, and asking God to give me a divorce. Now, what if God would have allowed us to get a divorce? I would not be having this proud mommy moment right now because my baby wouldn't have existed. I think about the many times I wanted to get an annulment when we first got married and once that period passed, I kept using the *D* word– divorce. At that time, I was the only one saying that I wanted a divorce; my husband was always the strong one. I would say that, and he would say that the devil is a liar, and we're not getting a divorce. Then, he would break out in a prayer, which used to make me so upset. I would say it again and again over the years, and he would either ignore it or pray.

One day the brother must have grown tired of hearing me ask for a divorce over the years, and maybe this day he was too tired to pray.

Again, I screamed, "I want a divorce."

He said, "Fine, I want one too. Go get the papers and I'll sign them."

It was as if my heart stopped. *Oh no,* I thought to myself. *Our marriage is really doomed. It's really over if he is saying he wants a divorce too.* I was too prideful to pray. So, as I walked away, I told him, "No, you get the papers, and I'll sign them." We would end the night like that and not speak to each other for days. Walking through the doors and hallways trying not to touch each other as we pass by. The struggle was real. Did you think that you and your husband were the only ones who did this? The devil wants you to think that. He wants you to think that your situation is so uniquely horrible that no other married couple is going through it; therefore, you should call it quits. How do I know? I've been there done that, and I don't want to ride that *woe is me, my life sucks, and our marriage is miserable* train anymore. Get off while you can, sis, and enjoy your marriage. Stop looking for fault, and the bad because the devil is going to make sure you find it. Instead, look for the beauty in your life and in your marriage, and God will make sure you find it.

Didn't the Lord make you one with your wife? In body and spirit you are his. And what does he want? Godly children from your union. So guard your heart; remain loyal to the wife of your youth. "For I hate divorce!" says the Lord, the God of Israel. "To divorce your wife is to overwhelm her with cruelty," says the Lord of Heaven's Armies. "So guard your heart; do not be unfaithful to your wife. (Malachi 2:15-16, NLT).

Every time I wanted to quit or reach a point where I had enough, this scripture would ring in my ear. I would kind of roll my eyes and ask God why I couldn't get a divorce because other people I know did it, and they are doing just fine. Some even seem happier with their new spouse. Why do they get an out and I don't? God would tell me that there are consequences to getting a divorce, and I didn't want that for my life. One time I remember God telling me:

What if I would have gotten down off the cross? What if I said the beatings were too painful and the Sins of the world were too hard to bear. Where would this world be Kat? I would pout like a little five-year-old and respond, *Daddy, this hurts! Please just take the pain away, I can't take any more. I feel myself breaking. I don't know who I am anymore. Is there more to me than just being a wife and mother? What is my purpose? Why am I still here?* I would shoot out the questions, and would sometimes only hear silence. *GOD, GOD do you hear me? Please, God, I need to hear you.* I would cry until there were no more tears left to cry, at least for that night.

I remember feeling stuck some days. I had quit my job a few times, and each time my husband was left to carry the load. We would have some good days followed by some hard days. Looking back, they were never really bad days, just hard days. There were times when I didn't want to change. There were times when I saw no change in him, or times when we would be on one accord all in love with googling eyes then the kids would act up. We would get frustrated and take it out on each other. BOOM! Just that quick satan had stolen our joy and we were too distracted with bills, finances, work, church, kids, school, or life to even realize it. Sometimes we did see the enemy, and we would go into spiritual warfare. Other times we were too drained to fight. In those moments it seemed like we just couldn't catch a break. We were drowning in a sea of doubt, fear, and unbelief. Sure, we knew what to do; we're Christians, right? Sometimes, we would yell and scream at each other on our way to church, praise the Lord in church, and then yell and scream at each other on the ride back home from church. Poor kids would be right in the backseat, quiet and taking mental notes that they would later share with us. During our alone time, I would say to my husband, "I just can't keep doing this anymore. I'm tired of pretending like we're great when we're falling apart. I want a divorce. I don't want to be with you anymore. I'm not in love with you, and I don't know if I ever loved you at all." Yes, ladies, I hate to admit it, but I let those harsh words come out of my mouth and fall to my husband's ear so many times. It's not that I wanted to leave to be with another man; that wasn't the case. Shoot! I just wanted to be free. I wanted out of the marriage and that was it. Thank God, in my time of emotional foolishness, my husband did not pack his bags and leave. So often emphasis is on the man leaving, but lately, I've been witnessing the woman calling it quits.

However, wives, we must stand in the gap for our marriage. We must watch and pray (Matthew 26:41). We must humble ourselves and turn from our wicked ways so God can heal our lands, which is our home (2 Chronicles 7:14). I encourage you to stay on the wall like Nehemiah. Don't give up just yet. You need to wait until you know that you have done absolutely all you could do to make your marriage work. Even when you reach that point, still give it to the Lord and let Him take you further.

Remember, I started this chapter off by quoting the scripture, "God hates divorce" (Malachi 2:15-16, NLT). This doesn't mean that He'll hate you and disown you if you get a divorce. No, God loves you no matter what! What this is saying is that He hates the act of getting a divorce because He knows the pain that it will cause to the family as well as to the heart and mind. It's just like if your children do something, like tell a lie. We hate when they lie to us, but that doesn't mean that we hate them as a person. We still love them, will guide them through life, and will still be there for them because they are our children. Not liking when they lie to us has nothing to do with our love for them in particular. We don't like the sinful act in which they partake, but we will forever love them. That's how God is with divorce. He doesn't like the sinful nature of divorce and how the separation of the union can cause damage to the family for generations to come. The husband and wife don't just feel the sting of divorce, but the children and grandchildren do too. The same goes if the marriage is healthy or unhealthy. This is why it's imperative that we choose our mates wisely. Even if you feel you haven't chosen wisely, there is still time to make the best of your marriage. Furthermore, it is our duty to teach our children to follow God's leading when choosing a spouse because love itself will not carry a marriage for a lifetime. Only prayer and God, being both the center of your lives and the head of your marriage, will carry you through.

CHAPTER 6: ACCEPT THE LIFE THAT GOD HAS GIVEN YOU

For I know the thoughts that I think toward you, saith the Lord, thoughts of peace, and not of evil, to give you an expectant end (Jeremiah 29:11, KJV).

There was a point when I didn't like my life. I didn't understand it. I didn't see the good in it. I was miserable and angry with God for giving me, what I thought at that time, was an unfair life. *Why me?* I asked God this question nearly every day. This was not the life I had planned for myself. Married with six kids, blended family drama, struggling, and barely making it. At one point in time, we were homeless living at a local hotel. From there, we went to stay with a family member. For a whole year, my family of eight did not have a home to call our own. I didn't understand how a couple like us got here. We were young and married, and we loved to serve God with our whole hearts. We taught our kids about having a relationship with the Lord. We also conducted bible teachings with them at home and made sure they were involved in church activities. We asked God how we ended up here.

At times, I didn't feel loved by my husband, and neither did he feel respected and loved by me. My heart would dislike and love my husband all in the same breath of a second. If you have ever felt this way, you may have asked yourself,

Why did God allow me to get married if He knew it was going to be like this? Why if He knew there were going to be days when our hearts would not be in it? Why did God put us together if He knew most of our marriage would be full of arguments, miscommunications, judgment, cold

shoulders, stonewalling, and silent treatments? Small talks about the weather could end up with us both expressing aggressive anger without either one of us knowing where the turning point of the conversation had occurred. How did we get to not talking for the rest of the night when we started out talking about the weather and the local news? Why is communication and intimacy so complicated? Why didn't God just let us marry someone else? Would our lives have been different? Would it be full of love, joy, fun and peace?

I just didn't understand! Was God even listening to me? Did He even care that I was hurting? Was God just like my natural father who could care less about what I was going through? Why wasn't God answering me? Why was He taking me through this? Does God even love me? *Does God even love me?* If He does, why does He love me? Shoot! It's hard for me to love me sometimes.

I would ask God these questions over and over again almost every day. I just didn't see the beauty in my life. I couldn't make sense of it. One reason was because my husband and I had received full custody of his two children that he had before we were married. They were taken from their mother and given to us to raise until she was back on her feet. We went to court a few years ago, and my husband reluctantly released them back over to their mother. She and I never really got along and didn't see eye to eye. I didn't and still don't like how she carries herself as a woman, nor do I agree with her parenting style and the way she's raising my bonus children. Over the years, she has been very disrespectful, distasteful, and she lacks much-needed tact and self-discipline. I've been with my husband for nearly fourteen years, and we still haven't seen a positive change in her behavior. Sadly, even after her kids were taken from her, it didn't change her behavior.

In addition to her disrespectful tantrums, my oldest son's father would begin sneak attacks here and there. Whenever he felt he wasn't getting his way, he and his wife would decide to take me back and forth to court. Unfortunately to this day, he too has not changed. However, what has changed is my need to set boundaries in my life. I no longer feel that I have to respond to their dramatic episodes, instead; I give it to God and let him handle the rest. I now know that God loves me tremendously and everything that I went through wasn't to break me; it was to build me. It was to make me better and build my character. The trials that I have endured during my marriage and from raising children have caused me to become bolder and gain more wisdom. I know my worth and value in Christ. I no longer give people who have ill-will intentions towards my family and I or who are blatantly disrespectful access to me. Having contention with someone gives that person too much of my time and energy. Now don't get me wrong. Some issues I will address, but it's on my terms depending on if I feel like it's worth my time, energy, and wisdom. If I think it's worth it, I'll address it; if I don't, then I won't. I've learned you have to let a fool be a fool, while you pray and keep your cool.

You can only imagine how stressful our lives were. We are a young God-fearing couple with a blended family that consists of six kids. There was baby daddy drama from my side, and baby mama drama from my husband's side. Some days my husband and I would be on one accord fighting the devil together in spiritual warfare, and other days it seemed like each other was the enemy. When it was good, it was good, but when it was bad, it was bad. Those times got the best of me. I would forget about the good days and zoom in on the bad days. I would forget about family trips, family game night, making family forts and tents out of blankets, and eating popcorn while watching a movie until we all fall asleep in the living room. I would forget about when my husband, who makes the best pancakes in the world to me, would get up some mornings asking who wants pancakes and the kids would scream "Meeeeee!!!" I would forget about how every day the kids would run and scream when their dad came in from work as if they didn't just see him earlier that day. I would forget about date nights and how faithful my husband and I have been to each other. I would forget about how much we both love the Lord. I would forget about how much we agree on and highlight the things we did not agree on. I would forget about how much I just love being next to him, even if I'm just sitting on the couch with my head on his chest listening to his heartbeat. I would forget about the times that he would leave for work and would call me as soon as he pulls off and tell me how much he genuinely missed me already. I would tell him that I missed him too. When we were at odds, all of that would go out the window, and all I could see at that moment, all the enemy allowed me to see, was my pain from all the arguments. I would focus on the silent treatments and disagreements in which we had recently partaken. Thank God we didn't deal with infidelity because that's a whole different type of warfare. However, we could take the smallest disagreement and just blow it up to the extreme. We would try not to argue in front of the kids, and guess what? We did. People would say just don't argue in front of the kids, go in another room or something. That didn't work because we would be so loud that the kids would hear us anyway. Ashamed, we

46

would ask our kids if our behavior had caused them to want to get married or not? They would say they still want to get married, but they don't want to argue with their spouses as we do. The older ones would reluctantly answer the questions, or try to avoid answering the question out of respect for us. But those little bold ones, born under the covenant, would drag their little voices and say that we argue almost every day and they can't take it anymore. In my mind, I would think, *Shut up. Y'all don't even know what love is yet, let me see how you are when you get in a relationship*. Yet, I would swallow those words and keep them hidden in my mind. I would say the nice things that a mommy is supposed to say. I let them know that we are trying to teach them to do better than we did. No one taught us how to be married. We had to learn on our own from the Holy Spirit, but they have an advantage because they have seen us struggle, fight the enemy, and be victorious. We could now guide them so they won't make the same mistakes we made.

We were arguing about the little things. Half of the time, by the end of the argument, I didn't know what we were arguing about, or how the argument got started. We were just arguing; going at it. As I began to grow in what I will and won't tolerate, I began setting boundaries for how far I will go with a conversation. I began setting boundaries not only with people outside my home but with my marriage as well. As soon as I sensed an argument, I would just shut down mid-conversation because I could just feel myself boiling, and I didn't want to get out of character. Because of the level of emotion that comes behind an intimate relationship, my husband is the only one that can get my blood pumping so that I would cuss him out before I knew it. Then I would have to pray, repent, and ask God to forgive me. I would ask

God to cleanse my mouth, my heart, my mind, and my emotions concerning my husband. I would be so upset with myself because I'm a Child of God and I know better. Anybody else can say what they have to say, and I would reply without one curse word, walking away after I said my peace. However, my husband can push buttons that no one else can push and vice versa. In an argument, I would tell him that he had gone far enough, and he would just keep going. On the contrary, he would tell me the same, but I would keep going until every last one of his buttons was pushed. Then BOOM! Before you know it after one of us had warned the other person who didn't yield, here comes an explosion of emotions and built-up aggressive anger. After the massive blow-up, we would both go to our individual area and cry out to the Lord, and ask Him to forgive us. One of us would make an attempt to rectify the situation the next day, but there would still be tension in the air that the whole house could feel. The tension was suffocating our joy. I found myself growing tired of going through this rat race of pain. It was like an emotional rollercoaster, as one songstress stated. There were ups and downs, twists and turns. I was emotionally and physically drained. I couldn't take it anymore. This wasn't love! Was this how our marriage was going to be for the rest of our lives? No, I want out! I can't do this! This is not healthy! The kids can't keep seeing us argue like this. We're not setting a good example of a healthy marriage. It's taking a toll on our bodies. Both my husband and I were feeling sick. We went to the doctor only for them to say they didn't see anything wrong other than stress. Stress? I'm too young for this crap.

I was working a full-time job at the time, making more money than I had ever made in my life. My boss and coworker were getting on my nerves. So, I would be stressed out at work. Then I would come home and be stressed out. I had no break. I would go from one stressful situation to another stressful situation. I'd wake up some days and before I could open my eyes good, tears would begin rolling down my face because I didn't want to go through another painful, stressful day. Sometimes I would pull up in the parking lot at my job and have to sit for a minute wiping tears and giving myself the daily pep talk about how we needed the money for bills. I just needed to go in and do what I needed to do to get through the day. When my shift was over, I would drive home, pull in my driveway and do the same thing. For my mornings going to work, I would sit in the parking lot for a minute and play a gospel song or two to prepare my mind before I went in. Then, on the way home, I would listen to a message to prepare me for my home life. I would sit in my driveway, and the tears would roll down my face. I would think to myself:

I don't want anybody asking me what's for dinner because I don't feel like cooking. I don't have the energy. I'm drained. I spent all my energy at work trying to make sure my face and body language didn't read "I don't want to be here. I'm only here because my bills need to be paid."

When I got home, I would sit in the driveway praying that my husband had cooked, and on most days, he did because he got home before me. He got off at 2 pm and made it home about 3:30 pm after picking up all the kids from school. I would drop them off in the morning because I had to be at work later than he did, and he got off early enough to get all the kids. We had a nice schedule that worked for us and around the kids' school schedule. My mother-in-love had taught my husband how to be a domesticated man, so he knew how to cook, clean, take care of the kids, put a ponytail in the girls' hair, change diapers, and do laundry. He had a lot of brothers and sisters, so their mom taught them how to cook and clean no matter their gender. I grew up with just me and my two brothers. My oldest brother was killed when I was fifteen, so it then just became me and my younger brother, who's about eight years younger than me. My mom loved to cook; it's her gift. So, there was no need for me to cook. I cooked the basics when I was younger, like hotdogs and noodles whenever my mom told me to fix my little brother and me something or I would warm up leftovers. Because my mom cooked, and I was the oldest and only girl, I had to do the dishes all the time. I grew up hating doing the dishes. As for cooking, of course when I got older and on my own, I had to learn how to cook. I have my mother and my grandmother's (Big Ma) genes in me, so I know how to cook. I can cook dishes from many cultures because I love to eat. I'm always trying new dishes: southern comfort food, African food, Thai, Ethiopian, Japanese (sushi is one of my favorites), and more. Give me a recipe, and I'll cook it and make it taste delicious. So I can cook. However, one thing I didn't inherit from my mom and my Big Ma was their passion to cook. Oh, I hate cooking, especially since all my children have allergies and recently my husband has had a low tolerance for foods he used to eat and love. Now that he's older, he can't have certain things as much. So, I always have to make several versions of one dish because one person can't have cheese, another person can't eat tomato sauce, and this one doesn't eat meat. By the time I get in the kitchen to cook, I'm overwhelmed with how many versions of simple mac and cheese I have to make just on a regular weeknight. So, cooking dinner at my

50

house is always a hassle. To top off the fact that I hate cooking anyway, I'm not fortunate to have the simplicity of making one meal that my whole family can eat. Even an easy pizza night is a struggle because we have to order three different pizzas, or depending on our budget that day, I have to give up wanting to eat meat that night. Because one kid is a vegetarian and can't have tomato sauce, we get a white sauce veggie pizza, which is delicious by the way. Then for the kids that can't have dairy, we get a Hawaiian BBQ chicken pizza without the cheese. Yes, they make pizza this way. You just have to find a pizza place that will. It took a while to figure this out, and a long explanation to pizza places that put cheese on everything. We looked weird to workers at the local pizza joint, asking for a pizza but telling them to hold the cheese, but hey, we got tired of our kids feeling left out not eating pizza so we figured something out. Now the kids are happy when we order pizza. The local pizza joint knows who we are and makes the pizza to our liking without any questions now. My life couldn't be simpler, right? My husband and children say I always tease them. I would find a new recipe and get excited about cooking it. I would make it, they would love it and say that I need to make that again. Nope, I tried it to see if I could do it, mission accomplished, the experiment is over. My husband would say, that I make all this good stuff, tease him and the kids, and then don't cook it again or have to wait a long time before I would cook it again. I hate cooking; it's too much. I prefer instant mashed potatoes, steamed vegetables, and baked chicken breast, the simple stuff. All of that standing over the stove for hours isn't for me. I've made a homemade apple pie before with a homemade crust, but why do I need to do it all the time when I can buy a perfectly good already made apple pie from the store? Earlier during the pandemic, we wanted hamburgers for dinner, we had meat and no buns. So, I said I'll just make some hamburger buns from scratch. I looked up a recipe on the internet, got out my flour, butter, yeast, and the other ingredients I needed to make some dough. I put those bad boys in the oven and *wallah*! We had some soft fluffy huge hamburger buns, and we ate hamburgers that night. My husband and kids said that those were the best hamburger buns ever. They were so soft and fluffy, and they wanted me to make them again. "Ugh, no! Why would I do that when I can buy it from the store?" That would always be my reply, but I digress.

As I sat in my driveway, I would sit there hoping he had cooked, and most likely he did. I was miserable. I was depressed and didn't know it. I hid my pain very well. No one outside of my home knew what I was going through. I felt broken, empty, out of love, and stuck. How did I get myself in this mess, and how can I get out was all I thought about at the time? I eventually quit my job. I decided that I could not fight both wars. I didn't have the strength to go into spiritual warfare for both my job and my home. I decided that since my destiny was connected to my marriage and children, I would put in the necessary work to get my home in order.

When I first quit my job, I felt free, but once I received my final paycheck from my employer and bills were due, I quickly started second-guessing my decision to quit. Not because I missed working there, but because we needed the money. However, shortly after I quit, the pandemic happened and my kids had to do remote learning. Because I was not working, I was available to be there when they needed me the most. At this point, I stop resenting my decision to leave my job because I had seen firsthand how God would work things out for your good. Yes, the job that I worked for went into work from home mode like the rest of the world, but who knows how stressed out I would have been trying to work from home, cook three meals a day and make sure that my kids were getting the proper attention and help that they needed from me during that time. I went from resentful to grateful. I told the Lord that even if I did make a mistake, He turned it around for my good.

It was during these times that I began to see that my life is really blessed. I had the opportunity to spend more time with my children. I was able to see how cool they were and their uniqueness. I was blessed to spend some much-needed quality time with my husband too. It showed me how much we really love each other, and that we actually have a good peaceful relationship. We both had a chance to sit and think about the many arguments we had had in the past, and we realized that our worst arguments came when we let outside things interfere. When we had no outside stresses, we were good. We were all lovey-dovey, gazing into each other's eyes. When was the last time you and your hubby did an evaluation of your marriage? Could it be like ours? Are there outside stresses that are hindering your relationship? Then you may have to do what we have now begun to do. Set boundaries and prioritize your marriage and each other, even when it comes to your children. Yes, your children are your priority, but they don't have priority over your spouse because one day they will move out and have a family of their own. You don't want that time to come and you and your husband realize that you didn't invest in your marriage and have now grown apart, rather than grown closer together.

I have to admit, as I began to get closer to God, my eyes started to be open to the beauty in my life, rather than all my problems; looking back wasn't as bad as I perceived it at the time. I have a God-fearing, fine specimen of a man who loves, honors, and is faithful to me. He will shout it from the mountain top that I am his good thing. I have children who love and respect me and are well-behaved. I have a Father in Heaven who loves me and gives me purpose. What more could a woman ask for? I had to wake up and appreciate the roses growing in my own backyard. Those roses are my husband and children, and the backyard is my heart. I used to blame the Lord for what I thought was a horrible life. Now, I can't thank him enough. God didn't take me out of the situation. Instead, He gave me grace, appreciation, love and a new perspective for the situation that I was already in.

CHAPTER 7: THE DEVIL WANTS YOUR MARRIAGE

"The thief cometh not, but for to steal, and to kill, and to destroy: I am come that they might have life, and that they might have it more abundantly" (John 10:10, KJV).

The devil not only wants your marriage, but he also wants your future and your legacy. There is no doubt about it and no guessing that the devil absolutely hates marriage with a passion. This shouldn't be a surprise seeing that he enjoys the things that God hates and hates the things that God loves. For example, God hates divorce (Malachi 2:15-16), but the devil finds joy in tormenting a married couple until they quit, especially a kingdom couple. He gets a kick out of trying to prove God *wrong*. As soon as a Christian couple gets a divorce, I can imagine the enemy just laughing and saying, "I told you so. I knew I could make them quit on their own destiny. Haha, weaklings." God, on the other hand, is saying "You did nothing satan because I'm going to work this out for their good" (Romans 8:28). The devil hates marriages, but God loves marriage. In fact, he created marriage to be a resemblance of Christ and the church. It is for this reason He charges the husbands to love their wife like Christ loved the church and gave up his life for her (Ephesians 5:25). Now, this doesn't mean that the husband will have to literally kill himself or die to prove that he loves his wife. No, that would be suicide, which is a huge sin for God. What this means, however, is that a husband is to die daily to the flesh for his wife, just as Christ died on the cross for His bride, the church. In the same manner that Christ gave up His life for the church, husbands are supposed to give up their old life for their bride. This is basically a change of mindset and behavior. For example, if a husband grew up in a house where they did not have healthy daily communication, they rarely talked about their feelings, and they didn't express themselves with pure love and affection, he's going to have a hard marriage when he marries a woman who craves love, affection, small talks and hugs unless he gets rid of his old mentality. A wife needs to feel love and wanted by her husband. If he's used to coming home from work, and watching the TV or playing a video game but never addresses her until he wants her to serve him by saying, "Honey, can you get me something to eat? Can you grab me the newspaper? Can you do this or that? Can we have sex?" then pretty soon she's not going to feel loved and wanted but rather used and lonely. When the enemy has you stuck in that feeling, he can play with your mind.

Most of the time the enemy will start with the wife, as she is the weaker vessel (1 Peter 3:7), just as he did to Eve in the garden of Eden. He convinced her to disobey God and her husband and engage in the very act that would take her and Adam away from the perfect life God had planned for them. That's the same trick the enemy still uses to this day. He bombards our minds with false imagination. We begin to think about a better life without our husband—a fun, more enjoyable life that doesn't involve arguments, disagreements, or stress. He paints a picture to us that we can make it on our own and the grass is greener on the other side. He deceives us into thinking that the separation or divorce will not really affect the kids if we just sit down as a family and talk about it. We even have the audacity to involve the kids by asking them silly questions like, "What do you think

about Daddy and Mommy not being together anymore?"
What a painful question to ask a child who can barely
comprehend that Mommy and Daddy are married. They
barely understand marriage, and now we want to
introduce them to the painful thought of divorce. The
enemy spent many nights and days planting these same
imaginations in my mind. I've wasted many thoughts and
I've wasted time thinking about life more abundantly
without my husband in the picture, just my kids and me.
If I can be really honest, there were some nights when
the kids would really get on my last nerve, and I would
say to myself that I'm going to leave them with their dad,
change my name and phone number, and move to an
island where no one can find me. I would just move
totally off the grid. It would just be me, myself, and I,
and God, of course. He's with me wherever I go.
Although there were some days while going through a
hard time, I would question if God was there at all.
Those were the days that I would find myself balled up
like a baby crying on the floor asking God to take the
pain away or take me away from the pain. No, I was
never suicidal. However, some days the pain of life
would be so unbearable that I would question my
existence. I would cry out, "Lord, why do you have me
here?" I wasn't just unhappy with the hard times that I
was going through with my husband. I was also
experiencing rough times with my family, friends,
church, coworkers, and just life in general. I would try to
explain my issues and feelings to my husband, and when
he didn't respond in the way I expected him to respond,
I would be further devastated than when I initially came
to talk to him. I would isolate myself, and then the
enemy would whisper crap in my ear. At the time, I
didn't know it was crap. I thought that they were my

own thoughts until I read Joyce Meyer's book *Battlefield of the Mind* where she writes about thinking about what you're thinking about (which I talk about in the next chapter). She mentions how all our thoughts are not our thoughts. Some thoughts come straight from the enemy's mouth. I would always hear the scripture, and even quote it, saying "Casting down imaginations, and every high thing that exalteth itself against the knowledge of God, and bringing into captivity every thought to the obedience of Christ" (2 Corinthians 10:5, KJV). Yet, I never really knew what it meant. Even though I was using it in my prayers, I didn't know its full meaning. That is until I read her book. I got an understanding of that scripture and I realized that I didn't have to accept every thought that came to mind. If I was thinking about my husband and I being happier with someone else, or if I thought about living alone with my kids and not my husband and feeling free from stress, this was a false image that I needed to cast down. It was false because it wasn't my truth. My truth was that I was still married and lived with my husband and kids. Any thought contrary to that was not my reality and thereby, it was false. Additionally, the word of God says that God hates divorce, and what God has joined together let not man put asunder (Malachi 2:16, Mark 10:9). So, if I'm having thoughts of me being happily single, I have to cast that down because it is an imagination. Imaginations are not real; therefore, it's not true. The truth is that my husband and I are still together. So, any vision, thought, or played-out drama scene in my mind that depicts any one of us in another relationship is a false imagination that needs to be cast down. The second part of that scripture says, "Cast down false imagination and anything that exalts itself against the word of God." If I keep hearing or saying that I need to get a divorce, that thought, imagination, or dream has now exalted itself against the word of God that says God hates divorce. If God told you to marry your spouse, and you know you heard it as clear as day, then why would God then come back and tell you to get a divorce, when He Himself says what God has joined together let no man put asunder. He would then be contradicting Himself, which is not biblical truth. Because the Bible I read says that "God is not a man, that he should lie; neither the son of man, that he should repent: hath he said, and shall he not do it? or hath he spoken, and shall he not make it good?" (Numbers 23:19, KJV). So, if you're saying you know for sure that God told you to get married to your husband, then turn around when times get tough and say that God is telling you to break the conventional vow you made to Him and get a divorce, both can't be true. That is not how the Lord works. Somewhere in there, your flesh is working. Either you heard him say get married, and now you want out because it's not the paradise island you thought it would be, or God never told you to get married to your spouse in the first place. Maybe you went off an assumption and convinced yourself and the people around you that the Lord told you to get married when He in fact had no part in it. That was you and your flesh in agreement, not you and God. Now all hell is breaking loose, and it is not as fun as it was in the beginning when you were sinning with the man. Now you're married and you're screaming it's not the same as before you two got married. You're saying God is telling you to get a divorce. Something is not right sis, and you need to fast and pray to get rid of your flesh and really get your heart posture right to really hear what God has to say to you. He might tell you what He told me the many times I wanted to quit: You're being immature and stubborn, and enough is enough.

Yes, a lot of times when I went to God on my husband and asked God to change him, God would tell me that it was me who needed to change. He would take me to His word and tell me about myself. Sometimes I would be in tears, apologizing to my husband and telling him that I needed to change, then I would start hugging him. He would wonder what happened because I was just mad at him, and I would tell him the Holy Spirit just got on me. Don't worry. My husband has had the same type of corrections from God as I have had. That's why it's key to have God in your marriage, to show you yourself when you are the one that's wrong and need to get things back on track. Because let's just admit it, wives, the problem is not always our husband. Sometimes it is us. Occasionally, we know when we are allowing satan to use us to push our husbands' buttons, but we don't resist the devil or tell him to flee (James 4:7). We just go right on flipping at the mouth, and the next thing we know, we have said or done something we can't take back. God gives us a way of escape, even in our little marital quarrel. We would hear, *Don't say that. Watch your tone.* Yet, we say it and yell anyway. Then we want to cry to God when it leads to a painful argument. Wives, we have to do better about discerning the voice of God and following it. We also must learn to discern the voice of the enemy and tell him to flee.

Before I learned that all thoughts were not mine, and started monitoring my thoughts, I used to let the enemy run my thoughts and get the best of me. I constantly had thoughts of my husband being happy with someone else, and I mean I would really have thoughts of him being with someone else. I had some

60

made-up person in my mind that would literally bring me to tears thinking about it because it seemed so real. The one thing that I love about my marriage is that my husband and I have very open and honest communication. So, I would share these thoughts with him with tears rolling down my face and no reason whatsoever to believe that my husband was cheating. However, as soon as we got into an argument, the enemy would come right away and whisper to me:

He would be happier with someone else. You should divorce him so he can be happy, and you'll be happier by yourself. You don't need another man because you are not going to really know him well. You have kids and you don't want anything to happen to your kids, so you should be alone at least until the kids are grown. Even then, you don't want a man because then you'll worry about somebody touching your grandkids. So just remain single. If you remain single, you may run the risk of masturbating all the time because you want a man. You don't want to be one of those Christian single women who pretend to be content and blessed but behind closed doors, they are pleasing themselves. Your husband is going to marry someone more beautiful than you who will easily do all the things he begged you to do, and you may end up with a man who beats you all the time.

The thoughts would go on and on. I would entertain them and try to think up strategies of how not to get a man who would beat me by just dating men that I've known for a while. That way I would know their character and know they won't hurt my children. I would insecurely ask my husband if he wanted to be with women that I thought were beautiful and had something going for themselves. He would sincerely tell me that he only wants me and he's too afraid of God to even think about anyone but me. Lies. I would ask myself how could he not think about other people when I think about being with someone else or him being with someone else. Then an argument would erupt because I would accuse him of not being honest with his feelings when in fact he was being honest with me. I didn't want to accept that he loves me and only has eyes for me because the enemy would paint that false imagination so clear that it felt like it was real. Besides, I grew up hearing that all men were dogs and cheated. Even though I had a husband who I knew deep down in my heart did not cheat, those words that I heard as a child still rang in my ear, and I felt it was only a matter of time before he did. Again, I was never the jealous type hovering over my husband to see who he was talking to, but I did have moments of insecurities. I would tell him that if he felt he was going to cheat, I'd rather him leave me alone and let me go about my business. He would assure me that he wasn't going to cheat because he loved God, me, and our kids way too much to jeopardize our marriage. It took a minute for me to get that. Although I didn't believe that all men cheated, it was hard for me to believe that men could be in a long-term relationship and not have the desire to cheat or be with someone else. I always thought it was a cap on the number of years they can stay in a relationship and remain faithful. God had to really work on my heart and mind. God had to give me the courage to allow myself to love and be loved by my husband. Eventually, my thought process changed. I thought if God can give me the strength and the desire to be faithful to my husband then surely, He can do the same for my husband concerning me. I had to allow myself to trust him, just as he had to trust me too. I thank God for a praying man and a husband who covered me as his wife. I thank God that my husband was mentally stronger than me in that area because my negative thinking could have driven him to cheat. Some husbands and wives believe if their spouse thinks their cheating then they might as well cheat. Others wouldn't hesitate to get a divorce if their spouse said that they would be happier with other people. However, my husband, even in my ignorance at the time, would grab me and hold me, put my head on his chest, his hand on my head, and kiss the top of my head. I would be crying and trying to push away, telling him that he doesn't love me and he should just leave me. He would just squeeze me tighter and begin praying a covering over my mind, "satan take your hands off my wife's mind. We fight not against flesh and blood but against principality… We will not get a divorce! We will always remain faithful to each other and only have eyes for one another. My marriage is covered by the Blood of Jesus, and it will last forever in Jesus' name." He would pray and hold me for however long it took for me to calm down. By the end of his prayer, the thoughts would be gone, but the tears would still be flowing. With watery eyes, I would look up at him and thank him for praying for me because the thoughts were too strong, and I couldn't shake them. He would kiss me and tell me that we were going to be okay because God got us. Oh, the many nights that this has happened before I realized what was going on. This was before I got a hold of wisdom and power and before I started studying to show myself approved. Now I'm better able, with the help of the Holy Spirit, to attack those thoughts myself. If I get a negative thought that goes against my reality, I cast it down. I tell the devil he is a liar and to get thee behind me in Jesus' name. Sometimes I can shake it off immediately. Other times I have to keep praying until it's gone. If it gets too heavy for prayer alone then I know I have to kill the flesh by studying God's word more and/or fast and pray. Even the Lord said this comes by fasting and prayer (Matthew 17:21). The thoughts don't stop coming because the devil wants to kill, steal, and destroy you, your husband, your children, and especially your marital union. He wants to destroy your legacy. So, know that he's coming for you, but you must be prepared by putting on the whole armor of God:

> Finally, my brethren, be strong in the Lord, and in the power of his might. Put on the whole armour of God, that ye may be able to stand against the wiles of the devil. For we wrestle not against flesh and blood, but against principalities, against powers, against the rulers of the darkness of this world, against spiritual wickedness in high places. Wherefore take unto you the whole armour of God, that ye may be able to withstand in the evil day, and having done all, to stand. Stand therefore, having your loins girt about with truth, and having on the breastplate of righteousness; And your feet shod with the preparation of the gospel of peace; Above all, taking the shield of faith, wherewith ye shall be able to quench all the fiery darts of the wicked. And take the helmet of salvation, and the sword of the Spirit, which is the word of God (Ephesians 6:10-17, KJV).

It is especially important to use the helmet of salvation to cover your mind from those negative thoughts that the enemy tries to implant into your mind. You have to decipher your thoughts from the thoughts

of the enemy. You must study the Bible and allow the
Holy Spirit to lead you in all truth. When the devil comes
at you with a lie about your children, your marriage, your
husband, or even you, you can hit him with the truth of
God's word. The enemy is very strong, persistent,
cunning, slick, and smart. He knows the word and goes
to church every Sunday, even when we don't. Don't
think that you can come at him in your own strength.
You're going to need the Holy Spirit to help you defeat
him in every area of your life. You have to allow the
Holy Spirit to give you a strategy to defeat him, or else
you're doomed. Don't let pride make you think that you
don't need God because you do, especially if you want
your marriage to work. God must be the glue that bonds
you and your husband together, or else it will be easy for
the enemy to come in and tear it apart. Satan doesn't
have to use other people to help him do it. He doesn't
have to use anyone but the two of you. He will have you
so full of yourself and stuck in your old ways that you
will refuse to put in the work to change to make your
marriage better. Trust me! He's done it time and time
again. He has convinced people to leave good marriages,
where there were no infidelity or abuse involved but just
pure hardened hearts and stubbornness. Some of those
people look back and regret getting a divorce, or they get
a divorce and act like they're still married by still doing
for one another like they never got a divorce. The enemy
makes them think they were better off as friends. That's
a lie. Even after years of divorce, they still allow the
enemy to speak to them. Our court system has made it
so easy to get a divorce. People can divorce over
irreconcilable differences, which allows people to get a
divorce just because they can't get along. It's not because
a spouse cheated or was abusive. It's because they just

couldn't agree on what color to paint the kitchen and the argument lead to another which lead to another, and they don't want to put in the hard work to fix it. They both think it's *easier* to just throw the whole marriage away, get a divorce, and possibly start over with someone new.

Please don't misunderstand me when I say divorce is not an option. I do not condone anyone staying in a marriage that is abusive in any way or in a marriage that has dealt with infidelity over and over again. My only suggestion for you as a wife, in these types of situations, is that along with the guidance of the Holy Spirit, you also need to seek natural help as well. You may need to seek out a professional counselor or find programs that help battered women and their children get to safety if that applies to you. God will not punish you for leaving a potentially harmful situation, especially when He sees all and knows all. In these types of cases, the decision to leave or stay is between you and God, and NO ONE can make that call for you. If you need the National Domestic Violence Hotline, call 800.799.SAFE (7233) or go to the website https://www.thehotline.org/.

Finally, brothers and sisters, whatever is true, whatever is noble, whatever is right, whatever is pure, whatever is lovely, whatever is admirable—if anything is excellent or praiseworthy—think about such things (Philippians 4:8, NLT).

Joyce Meyer writes, "Thinking about what you're thinking about is very valuable because satan usually deceives people into thinking that the source of their misery or trouble is something other than what it really is. He wants them to think they are unhappy due to what is going on *around* them (their circumstances), but the misery is actually due to what is going on *inside* them (their thoughts)" (*Battlefield of the Mind*, 1995). As I mentioned in the last chapter, I didn't know that the devil was using my mind as his own personal playground. Thoughts would come and I would just run with that thought. When I was going through my time of depression, I didn't know what the heck was wrong with me. My husband and kids would be sitting in the front watching television as a family when I came home from work, and I would come in slamming doors. The room would get quiet and my husband would look at me while the kids tried to avoid looking at me. I could tell that all of them were wondering what was wrong with me. I would go to my room, lock the door and start bawling. I didn't even know what I was crying about. Even if I had a good day at work, and my husband and I didn't argue the previous day or the kids didn't get on my nerves, I would still come home and cry. I didn't know what was wrong with me. I would ask myself why I was crying, and the more I thought about my life, the more I cried.

No one outside of my home knew what I was going through because I hid my pain well. The good old "Blessed and highly favored" response when the church folks ask how I was doing kept them off my back when I was at church. If anyone else asked how I was doing, whether it was a stranger at the store or a co-worker, I would hit them with the good old "I can't complain" line. I kept it moving while saying to myself, *I got a whole heck of a lot to complain about, starting with this marriage— my entire life to be exact.* I never wanted to bore people with the *Woe is me* conversation, and truly I didn't think people really cared. People ask you how are you doing, but do they really give you the time to answer? That question has now become so routine to people. I really didn't think people cared enough to listen, and to be honest, I didn't know if I could get through the story without crying. I looked at myself as a strong woman who thought that everybody didn't need to see me cry. I had perfected holding back my emotions just long enough to speak briefly and any conversation longer than that was going to showcase a river of tears. I did not want to lose my cool in front of just anybody, so I held it all in, isolated myself, and silently dealt with my own fears and tears because I didn't trust anyone with my emotions, not my husband and not even God.

I entertained the thought of divorce every time it would come out and play with me. I would watch my marital life go by in the blink of an eye in my mind. It played over and over in my mind like a broken record. Marriage cannot be this difficult. Raising children cannot be this hard. My grandmother, whom I affectionately call Big Ma, had eight kids that are all alive and doing well. They are all in their right minds, and they are not in jail. How did she do it without losing her mind or having a nervous breakdown? I'm my grandmother's namesake, nickname and all, so I wanted to be just like her when it came to having kids. She had eight children and I, too, wanted eight because I loved our large family gatherings, and I wanted the same for my life. Plus, with eight kids, whenever my Big Ma and granddaddy needed something, all of their kids, grands, and great-grands would pitch in to help. My grandmother lives in another state, and one time when she got sick, all eight of her kids took a week or two off work to head down to take care of her. Some of the grands were grown and old enough to take a turn too. So, with such a large family, she had people in rotation to take care of her for about three months, which was long enough for her to get back up on her feet and take care of herself. She didn't have to worry about strangers coming in because her kids and grandkids stepped up. My granddad didn't have a lot of pressure on him either when it came to trying to take care of her. She is now in her late eighties and is doing very well for herself. She's in her right mind and can take care of herself. She still cooks for herself without any assistance. She lives in her own home, and she doesn't need to be put in assisted living. In fact, she told us we better not put her in adult care. She wants to stay in her own place without anybody telling her what to do. I don't blame her. Anyway, with the way my aunts and uncles spoil my Big Ma, I could tell that she raised them right. They love, cherish, and honor her very much. Because of that, I wanted a big family too. I want to train my children in the way they should go so when they get older, they will not depart from it (Proverbs 22:6, KJV). Again, like my grandmother, I wanted eight kids. I said that up until I started having kids; then I decided that I would stop at four. I had my two bonus babies, too, which equals out to six and that's close enough to eight for me. I said all that to say my Big Ma became my lifeline during those dark moments in my life. She didn't know it, but she was. We didn't talk every day, but when we did talk, I felt like she was the only one who truly understood how overwhelmed and stressed I was with trying to raise many children, be married, work, and have a family all while trying to learn on your own. She too didn't have anyone to show her how to do marriage right. She lost both her parents when she was a child and learned most of the things she knew on her own. Nevertheless, it seems like she always knew when to call and check on me. She would call and ask me how I was doing, and I would say I was doing fine, knowing I wasn't but I didn't want to worry her. She could always sense it was something bothering me because of that mother/grandmother's intuition. I believe it was the Holy Spirit dropping her some hints. She would say no you're not I can hear it in your voice. With tears running down my face I'll swallow as to not give away over the phone that she had tugged on a soft spot in my heart and it made me shed tears. I'll gather myself just long enough so that I can make it through the call without boohooing. When she would get off the phone, I would soak up my pillow with tears. My Big Ma doesn't know it, but she saved my life. Depression, anxiety, nervous breakdown, stress, and overwhelming thoughts were all knocking at the door to my heart and mind. The crazy part was that I didn't even know that I was going through it, I couldn't pinpoint it. I had convinced myself that I was holding it together very well, especially to those on the outside looking in. However, those emotions were pounding so loudly that I thought that they were going to kick in the door to my heart, or in my case stop my heart from beating. That's just how bad it was. While talking to my Big Ma one day, she told me something that I had never known, and it freed me almost instantly. She revealed to me that my great grandmother, my grandfather but her husband's mother, had gone into the mental institution when my grandfather was about two years old and she never came out. My grandfather is the second to last child born of about eleven kids. My great-grandmother had just had her last child, baby number eleven for her, which was my granddad's baby brother. My Big Ma says the story is that people say it just seemed like her mind just left her. I believe my great-grandmother dealt with postpartum depression after having all those kids back to back like that, but back then they hadn't quite discovered it or knew how to properly treat it. When we got off the phone, I was so stuck on the words "she went into a mental institution and never came out. She just never came back to herself, they say." It was like it freed me instantaneously. I spoke into the atmosphere:

Oh devil, I see what you are trying to do. You are trying to make me have a nervous breakdown like you did my great grandmother. Well, not this one, not me. No other woman is going to raise my children but me. I refuse to let you take me out like that. You want a war, then let's go!

I was led by the Holy Spirit to start studying scripture about transforming my mind and to start eating on the word of God. The first book and devotion I got was *Battlefield of the Mind* by Joyce Meyer. In her book she talks about paying attention to the conditions of your mind and keeping it free, peaceful, and full of faith. Man, did this lady help set me free! Before reading her book and doing the devotion, I would just think a thought and run with it. She has a whole chapter about thinking about what you're thinking about. She talked about how some thoughts are not our own thoughts. Some are negative seeds planted by the enemy to torture you and make you give up on your God-given assignment. I had never thought about what I was thinking about. All my life I had assumed that anything I thought was a thought of my own. Here I am saved, sanctified, and filled with the Holy Ghost, as they say in the Pentecostal churches, and didn't know the devil can invade my thoughts. It didn't dawn on me that he was just that powerful against us. That's why we can't fight him with our own strength. We need the power of God and His anointing to destroy every yoke of bondage from the enemy. We cannot defeat satan on our own, and by our own name. Jesus Christ conquered death, hell, and the grave. Only by the name of Jesus will the devil flee. I ran across the scripture Philippians 4:7-9, which said,

> And the peace of God, which passeth all understanding, shall keep your hearts and minds through Christ Jesus. Finally, brethren, whatsoever things are true, whatsoever things are honest, whatsoever things are just, whatsoever things are pure, whatsoever things are lovely, whatsoever things are of good report; if there be any virtue, and if there be any praise, think on these things. Those things, which ye have both learned, and received, and heard, and seen in me, do: and the God of peace shall be with you (KJV).

I began to think about those things that were lovely and pure about my marriage, my husband, my children, and my life. I started seeing the beauty in my life, and my life wasn't that bad. It was actually good. I had six beautiful children, who were all unique with their own personalities. They were not a burden but a blessing. I started looking at my husband differently. Instead of waking up basically disliking him every day, I began to fall in love with him. Instead of making up reasons and plans to leave the marriage, I started looking for reasons to stay. You're going to find whatever you're looking for—good or bad. I started telling myself, *You're young and married to a man who loves God. He loves you. He's faithful to you, and he is so fine—Kat get it together.* Then the battle in my mind shifted its focus. Once I stopped seeing the bad qualities in my husband that made me feel like I could do better than him, I then started looking at his good qualities, and the enemy attacked and made me feel like my husband can do better than me. *You're not a good wife. He deserves someone better than you, who's going to serve him more and respect him. You should just leave so that he can be with a woman who's going to appreciate him. He's too fine to be with you. Look at you! You're cute, but you won't even fix yourself up.* I began my journey to get rid of those thoughts. I began diving into the scripture 2 Corinthians 10:3-5:

> For though we walk in the flesh, we do not war after the flesh: (For the weapons of our warfare are not carnal, but mighty through God to the pulling down of strongholds;) Casting down imaginations, and every high thing that exalteth itself against the knowledge of God, and bringing into captivity every thought to the obedience of Christ...(KJV).

In addition to studying what the word says about the mind and thoughts, God led me to get a spiritual mentor, whom I talk to often. She's a powerful woman of God and strong in her prophetic gift. She's a doctor by trade, but an awesome minister and a true daughter of the King. We've had many conversations where she had to get me back on track, many conversations of reassurance. She helps me with diving into the word by taking my day-to-day issues and providing responses with the word of God. Whenever I'm faced with a problem, she doesn't lean on her own understanding. She always says, "Well, let's go to the black and white Bible to see what it says because God's word doesn't lie." Could I have responded more godly? Could I have thought more godly? I thank God for her because I don't know if I would have come this far in my mental transformation without her. Transforming your mind by getting rid of old ways of thinking and doing things takes time and work. You can't do it alone. You need prayer partners to help you pray when you are too weak to pray for yourself. You need a God-fearing Kingdom mentor. You need someone sent to you by God who will have the patience and godly wisdom to war, pray, and intercede on your behalf. You need someone to give you godly counsel who will lead you closer to God the father. Please pray about who your mentor should be, and allow God to reveal the mentorship to both you and that person because changing your mindset is a serious thing. If you change your mind, then you can change the trajectory of your life. You don't want to give that responsibility to just anyone. I would suggest that you get someone who is more biblically grounded and more spiritually disciplined than you are. Pray for someone who believes in Jesus and the truth of His word as well as someone who helps you gain more clarity of your life through God's word. Seek God for help during your journey to transformation to a better version of yourself.

Lean not to your own understanding, and in all your getting, get an understanding (Proverbs 3:5 & Proverbs 4:7).

Pray without ceasing (1 Thessalonians 5:17, KJV).

Having an ongoing prayer life is imperative. Prayer, worship, and fasting are things you must have and must do in order to sustain a godly marriage. It is through prayer that you give God your pain, shame, embarrassment, disappointments, fears, doubts, sickness, confusion, loneliness, temptation, addiction, and lack. Prayer is when you give God everything. Prayer is when you thank Him for your wins and cry out to Him for your losses. Prayer is when you get the opportunity to commune with God. It's where you develop a relationship with God. It's dating God and getting to know Him. It's where you learn that He loves you. It's where He waits to sit with you and hear about your day. Prayer is where you learn that when you talk, God hears, listens, and answers you. Prayer is communicating with God on a personal or corporate level. If you want to sustain a godly marriage, built on God's biblical principles, then you must learn when and how to pray different types of prayers and how to pray without ceasing.

Prayer is the one communication that you can have anywhere and any time of day. You can say it aloud or think it in your mind. God hears you whether it's spoken words out loud, thoughts in our mind, feelings in your heart, or an aching groan that we have no words for. God hears us. God knows us so well that without saying one word aloud, He knows what we need and want. He knows our desires because He gave them to us. He knows our heart, whether our intentions are pure or wicked. He knows. God is a friend who is available whenever we call Him. He will never leave us or forsake us (Deuteronomy 31:6). The Bible also says, "Ask, and it shall be given you; seek, and ye shall find; knock and it shall be opened unto you" (Matthew 7:7, KJV). So, whatever you want or need, just ask God the Father, and in His timing, He will provide as He sees fit.

Moreover, you will need an ongoing prayer life because there will be times in your marriage when you may feel alone. In fact, did you know that you can be married and still feel alone? You can even be surrounded by lots of friends and family and still feel alone and unwanted. To be alone is to isolate yourself from others. It is the act of separating yourself from people so as to not be bothered by others or to distance yourself mentally, physically, and emotionally. You can be in a room full of people, yet still feel distant from everyone. This is because the enemy has tricked you. The devil has invaded your thoughts and has convinced you that you are lonely. It's in these times that developing a personal relationship with God the Father is pivotal for your growth, your healing, your mental state of mind, and your transformation. I can only speak from my own experience and what has caused me to get out of a place of loneliness. Things began to change in my life when I developed a closer relationship with God and accepted His love for me. Yes, I knew he cared for me, but I didn't believe God loved me. I compared His love for me to the love given to me by my natural father. In fact, earlier in my walk with Christ, I didn't call God, *Father*. I called Him God. I saw Him as a higher being from which I was distant. I thought that He was a selfish and unfair God who wanted me to suffer in order to be blessed. I thought that in me enduring suffering for faith's sake, I was somehow proving to God that I was worthy of a blessing. Because of this, I would pray and blame God if things still didn't go the way I wanted them to go in my life. I began to not trust God in certain areas of my life. I got tired of feeling like I was suffering for a blessing. Heartache and pain seem to just start coming at me from every direction–family, friends, marriage, children, and work. I mean everywhere. My circumstances had forced me to a place of isolation where I felt I could trust no one, not even my husband with my heart and emotions. It was in this lonely place that I found myself running back to God for healing and restoration. It was in this place that I learned that God is truly my Father and He loves me. I learned that He is not selfish, and He wants the best for me. His plans for me are good (Jeremiah 29:11). In this place, I found myself crying out to God. I'm telling you it literally felt like I was lying in the lap of the Lord, and He was rubbing my head telling me everything was going to be okay, daughter. To hear Him call me daughter made me realize that I was truly His child. After a few encounters like this, I began to become secure in God's love for me, and secure in who I am in Christ. I am a daughter to the most high God, my Father.

> Who shall separate us from the love of Christ? shall tribulation, or distress, or persecution, or famine, or nakedness, or peril, or sword? As it is written, For thy sake we are killed all the day long; we are accounted as sheep for the slaughter. Nay, in all these things we are more than conquerors through him that loved us. For I am persuaded, that neither death, nor life, nor angels, nor principalities, nor powers, nor things present, nor things to come, Nor height, nor depth, nor any other creature, shall be able to separate us from

the love of God, which is in Christ Jesus our Lord (Romans 8:35-39, KJV).

In addition, 1 Thessalonians 5:17 says, "Pray without ceasing" (KJV). That means to pray uninterruptedly and without omission. Pray uninterruptedly, meaning without a break. Find a quiet place and lay your issues before the Master's feet. Go somewhere where you can be alone with God to commune with Him, so He can heal your broken heart, correct you, or give you direction. Pray without omission, meaning don't leave anything out. Tell God everything! You may not be able to tell people about the good, bad, and ugly thoughts you are having towards your mate, but you can definitely tell the Lord. Besides, He already knows your heart and He knows what you're thinking. So, there is no sense in trying to hide anything from God. He sees all and knows all. He knows when you're hurting and when you're happy. He knows you better than you know yourself. Give Jesus a try, and watch Him move on your behalf.

But they that wait upon the Lord shall renew their strength; they shall mount up with wings as eagles; they shall run, and not be weary; and they shall walk and not faint (Isaiah 40:31, KJV).

When I was preparing for the "Wives on a Mission to Endure" Conference in 2021, the Lord gave me Isaiah 40:31 as the conference's scripture. Prior to then, I had never looked at this scripture in terms of marriage. However, once He revealed to me how it pertained to marriage, I was in awe. "They that wait upon the Lord shall renew their strength" (Isaiah 40:31, KJV), meaning that if married couples wait on God before they give up on their marriage, He will renew their strength. Couples should wait on God when they feel like throwing in the towel because things are no longer the same in their relationship. They should wait on God when they have had so many painful, unhappy days in their marriage that they just don't have the strength to be with their spouse another day. It's at this point that God is saying give your marriage completely to Him. God wants you to give every painful situation, every moment of betrayal, every heartbreak, lack of trust, times of unhappiness, and your need for growth all to Him. You have been moving in your own strength, and it has been weighing you down. You have become exhausted with even trying anymore. God says He knows that your days have seemed long and your nights have been hard, but He doesn't want you to carry the burden anymore. He wants you to look "To the hills which cometh your help, and your help comes from him" (Psalm 121:1-2, KJV). If you will allow Him to be your present help in your time of need, He can heal your broken heart and put the broken pieces of your marriage back together. You can't do it in your own strength. You have to allow Him to give you strength because the joy of the Lord is your strength (Nehemiah 8:10, KJV). God wants to give you your joy back. He wants to give you your peace of mind back, but you have to be brave enough to take it back from the enemy. The devil has taken so much from you and out of you since you've been married, and He has even convinced you that you made a mistake in marrying your husband. He has convinced you that you married the wrong person, and your life would be better without your spouse. He has convinced you to leave because it's never going to get better, but the devil is a liar. I prophesy that your later years with your current husband will be better than your former years, in the name of Jesus.

The next thing God revealed to me in that scripture was that "they shall run, and not be weary" (Isaiah 40:31, KJV). Running represents your youthful years in your marriage. This can represent the newness of your marriage as in when you two were newlyweds. Run and not be weary also represent the earlier years that you two spent raising kids and running around with the children to school events and extracurricular activities. Additionally, these are your working years, when the two of you are working hard outside the home to earn money to put food on the table and pay the bills. This could also be the time when one is going to work and the other is at home taking care of the kids and managing the home. Either way, the run is indicative of the busiest years in your marital life. This consists of raising the kids, having a career, going to school events, doing extracurricular activities, taking work trips, attending social events, furthering your education, and serving in a church. In these times, don't grow weary in your well-doing (Galatians 6:9). Simply put, do not get tired of each other and allow yourselves to grow apart. In all that busyness that life could and will bring you two, don't lose sight of God's purpose for your marriage, nor forget to put each other first and make the marriage a priority. Good marriages have fallen by the wayside due to this very reason. One or both spouses get so caught up in life outside the home, or so caught up in working to pay the bills, that they fail to invest the time and energy it takes to make the marriage healthy and strong. They put so much time into the kids and running around for the kids' events that they stop, or rather forget to date each other. Dating is so important in a marriage; it helps you to stay connected, and have intimate conversations away from the home and children. My husband and I noticed that we are most at odds with each other when we have failed to date and make our marriage a priority. This is key to making a marriage last. The devil has divided so many marriages with affairs because either the wife or the husband found comfort in talking to someone else other than their spouse because the spouse was too busy *working*. Don't allow satan to ruin your marriage like this. Cover your marriage, get out of your comfort zone, and begin to trust your spouse with your heart again. If you don't know where to start, start by praying and asking God, and He will direct you. Follow His still small voice, or the unction that He gives to you to do something amazing for your husband. My prayer is that in the running years of your marriage, you and your husband will not be weary, but that God will give you two new strategies to keep your marriage fresh, enjoyable, happy, loving, exciting, and everlasting.

Lastly, God showed me, "They shall walk and not faint" (Isaiah 40:31, KJV). According to the Merriam-Webster Online Dictionary, faint means to lose courage or spirit; to become weak. Walking, of course, is a slower pace than running. Walking represents slower times in your marriage. These are the times that you have been married for a while. The kids may be grown and out of the house, and you two are now probably empty nesters with grandchildren and great-grands. One or both of you have retired, and life has slowed down a bit. Well, actually a lot. My prayer is that in these slower years when you two are no longer running in marriage but are walking in the marriage, you don't get tired of one another or become too common with each other. I pray that you will never feel like you know each other so well that you get bored with each other. It is my prayer that you and your husband will be the number one and only student in each other's class of love, and the two of you will continuously see each other as a masterpiece to study. I pray that finding new ways to express your love to one another will become a lifetime of adventure and that you will journey through life together with joy and excitement. I pray that you will see the beauty in every situation and that you will quickly solve conflict with peace, understanding, and joy, thinking not just of yourself.

I pray that you two will always find ways to be enthusiastic about your marriage, each other, and your life together. We are always growing as individuals and as a couple. So, I pray that you both will always take the time out to repeatedly get to know the new version of each other because we are not the same as we were when we first became married. Goals and dreams change. Some people go from being an unbeliever to a believer of Christ and their whole perspective of life changes. Having children changes the way we think and do things. Many things can cause us to grow or not grow, and we have to be patient with each other in the growing process. The husband can be growing in one area and the wife in another, we must be patient and understanding of each other's growth. It's in these times that couples can feel like they are growing apart and need a divorce when in actuality all they need is more one-on-one time with each other or more patience and understanding for one another. My prayer is that before you throw in the towel, you take a course in "Getting to Know My Husband Again 101," and study the new version of your husband and see him for who he has become and not for who he was or what you keep trying to make him out to be.

In a nutshell, in the times of walking through your marriage, so that you will faint not, take a moment to sit back and study your man. Encourage him, and tell him how much you appreciate him for staying and that you recognize his growth. Plan a day where you can pamper and love up on him. Pray, and leave the rest up to God. See how your husband will show up differently, and watch as God shows up and shows out in your marriage.

CHAPTER 11: ENDURE: REMAIN IN EXISTENCE

And if one prevail against him, two shall withstand him; and a threefold cord is not quickly broken (Ecclesiastes 4:12, KJV).

Marriage is supposed to be permanent. It's supposed to be forever. That's the way God designed it. It's an earthly representation of Jesus and the church, which is His bride. You don't see Jesus divorcing the church, do you? So why do we do it? In Matthew 19:8, Jesus told the Pharisee, "Moses because of the hardness of your hearts suffered you to put away your wives: but from the beginning it was not so" (KJV). Marriage is what you make it, but I have to admit sometimes, or most of the time at least for me, marriage is hard. It's very difficult. Two people coming together as one seems easy when you're young, in love, dating, and having fun. What happens when the love fades and fun seems like a far-away memory? How do you get the endurance to last the test of time? What happens when all the cute and quirky things that your husband did while dating now become annoying? What happens when the once sexy specimen of a man you call your husband used to turn you on as soon as he came into the room, but now the very sight of him makes you roll your eyes and think to yourself, *If he only knew how much he gets on my nerves.* The very sight of him no longer gives you goosebumps and butterflies, but rather stomach aches and watery eyes. What do you do? How do you make it through those times? How do you last? Kat, how do you endure? What you do is get as close to God as you possibly can. You don't focus on getting the marriage together, but rather getting *your* relationship with God together. *You* invite the Lord back into your heart and mind and let Him lead and guide you into all truth.

Don't make the same mistake that I did in the middle of my marriage. I ran from Christ, and I did so while being a faithful churchgoer and serving in the church. You read that right. I was faithful in the church, and I was still running from the One who I was going to see every Sunday. A form and fashion, but denied the power thereof. I believed in God, but not every aspect of Him. I had known God to be a teacher, provider, and protector. I had seen Him move in such a way in my life. Yet, I had not seen His healing power at work in my life. Can He really heal my broken heart? Can He really heal my marriage? Can we really fall back in love with each other after causing each other so much pain and emotional damage? I really didn't know.

I mean, is there a step-by-step plan on how to stay married for a lifetime guaranteed out there somewhere? For example, if you want to be married for five years do this, ten years do this, and if you want to be married for a lifetime, you have to do x, y, and z. To be honest, you can read 50,000 books on how to make a marriage last. They could be hypothetical book titles such as "How to Save Your Marriage in 21 Days," "How to Change Your Spouse into a Better Man for You," "How to Be a Better Wife for Your Spouse," "How to Have and Effective Argument that Succeeds and Leads to a Better Marriage," "Life Without the Kiddos," or "How to Relearn Your Spouse." However, if your mind is made up about getting a divorce, it doesn't matter how many books you read or videos you watch. No one but the Holy Spirit can change your mind. No one but God can allow you and your husband to see each other differently and in the same way God sees you both. Deciding whether to stay married or get a divorce isn't easy but it's a simple answer; *make a decision!*

I know you were ready to get to the end of the book and read a clear sign on whether you should stay in your marriage or get a divorce. Some of you picked up this book as a last resort to solving your marital woes in hopes of a clear sign and a miracle that says *If your husband does this, stay. If he does this, leave.* To be honest, no one but the Holy Spirit can tell you that if you are willing to listen. We all are given a measure of faith (Romans 12:3), and it's up to your measure of faith and level of endurance whether or not you remain married or prematurely abandon your assignment and get a divorce. I pray that before you make that permanent move that you fast and pray about it, as to be led by the Holy Spirit and not your flesh. In the meantime, keep rocking my sister. Keep believing and keep praying because you may very well be a wife on a mission to endure. Bless you! May you be a wife guided by the Holy Spirit and not by your own feelings. Our feelings can sometimes lead us astray, but the Holy Spirit always guides us to all truth and to those things that are best for us. If the Holy Spirit is leading you, then keep walking, but if the Holy Spirit is not leading you, then I encourage you to turn back to Him before it's too late.

Dear Lord,

I thank You for every wife that picks up this book. It is my prayer that they receive an encounter from You while reading this book. Lord, give them the strength to endure. For you said in Your word that the race isn't given to the swift, but the one who endures to the end (Ecclesiastes 9:11, KJV). Help them not to quit. Not to quit on their marriage, themselves, their legacy, and most importantly not to quit on You. When the enemy comes in like a flood, remind them to put on the whole armor of God that they may withstand in the evil days, and so they may be able to stand against the wiles of the devil. Remind them that Ephesians 6:16 says "above, all taking the shield of faith, wherewith ye shall be able to quench all the fiery darts of the wicked" (KJV). So, Lord give them the faith to quench and extinguish ALL of the fiery darts of the wicked. Remind them of this scripture when they feel defeated. That Your word says that they shall be able to quench not some, but All of the fiery darts of the wicked. That whatever the enemy throws their way by faith they shall extinguish it. Lord, I pray that these women do not get weary in their well-doing. That while they are serving their families, they don't forget to take care of themselves. That they will remain pure in their thoughts and deeds toward people. That they will love, honor, and respect their husband. But they will also love, honor, and respect themselves. With that being said, they will not do things that will go against your character Lord, nor will they defile their marriage. That they will keep themselves pure and holy. That their husbands will wash them with the Word, showing no spot or wrinkle in them. That they may be presented to You as a glorious church. Remind them that they are the church; they are Your bride. And, they shall carry themselves as such.

Lord, help these wives to never lose sight of themselves nor sight of You. Give them the strength and the will to submit to their husband as he submits to You. Let their husbands have favor with man because he's a mighty man of God, fit for the Master's use. Let their marriage be sexually and emotionally satisfying, lacking no good thing from You Lord. If there is a wife reading this book who is in a marriage where her husband doesn't know You, but she as the wife does, bring her husband to You, Lord, so that he may take his rightful place in the home. Let her husband be a leader and not a dictator. Allow him to let You lead him, and not outside forces. Let him love, honor, and cherish his wife. May he not devalue her with his words and actions. May he honor her as the weaker vessel, and take care of her fragile heart. May he speak words that will uplift her and not tear her down. Lord, if there are wives reading this book, and they are in an abusive marriage, whether physically, mentally, emotionally, or spiritually, speak to her weary soul. Lord, no one but you can tell her to stay or go. You are the only one that knows the outcome of her situation. Let her be so anchored in You that she will hear You clearly and accurately about what to do in her situation. My sister is hurting, Lord, and secretly, depressed. Touch her right now Lord, and give her direction and strength. Restore her joy for the joy of the Lord is her strength.

Lord deepen our relationship with You and give us a thirst for Your word so that we may be able to properly manage our households. We need You, God, and we want more of You. Help us, Lord, for we cannot do this marriage assignment without You, and we definitely cannot go through this life without Your guidance. Your words say, "The steps of a good man are ordered by the Lord: and he delighteth in his way" (Psalm 37:23, KJV). So, guide our footsteps in our homes, on our jobs, our churches, in business, entrepreneurship, motherhood, womanhood, friendships, extended and blended family situations, educational endeavors, finances, social encounters, in our community involvement, and economically. If there is anyone deciding to relocate, Lord be in the move and guide them in their decision on what area to move to. Lord, we need your guidance in every aspect of our lives. Speak to us and through us Lord. Guide our tongues so that we won't be a foolish woman who tears down her house with her own hands (Proverbs 14:1). Let us be a Proverbs 31:26 woman, that when we open our mouth we shall speak wisdom and in our tongue will be the law of kindness. Tell us when to speak up and when to be quiet, and when the time comes give us the strength to do both.

Lord, we thank You for who You are in our lives. We thank you for being Abba Father. That when our natural fathers walked away, you stayed. Thank You, Lord, for never leaving us or forsaking us. Even when our mother, sister, brother, family, and friends abandon us, You are right there to console our aching hearts, and for that, we are forever grateful. Thank You for removing relationships out of our lives that meant us no good. Even when we wanted to stay and endure the pain and betrayal that they were inflicting on us, it hurt to walk away, but You gave us the strength to leave. You removed them, and You sent better. Thank You, Lord.

Lord, if there's a wife reading this and she does not know You, save her now Lord. Soften her heart that she may receive You, for Your word says the day You hear my voice harden not your heart (Hebrews 3:15). Let her know that You will take away the pain, hurt, shame and disappointments, and even the unwanted success. Lord, let her know that Your yoke is easy and Your burdens are light (Matthew 11:28-30). That if she confesses with her mouth and believes in her heart that Jesus is the son of God, and Jesus died and You, God, raised him from the dead, then she will be saved (Romans 10:9). Send godly women in her life to minister to her soul. Let her do away with ungodly counsel, lying tongues, gossip, and backbiting. Make her fresh and new. Transform her mind, so that she may be a new creature in Christ. If she has any friends steering her in the wrong direction, peacefully remove them. Send her godly friends, sisters in Christ, as their replacements, who will lead her closer to You. This is my prayer in Jesus' name, Amen!

OMG, I just wrote my first book! It's been a long time coming, but it is finally here. I could not have done it by myself. I first want to thank God for giving me the health, strength, and the mind to write. Whenever I felt I had nothing left to say, the Holy Spirit stepped in to give me the words that I needed to write this book. I thank you God for always giving me chance after chance to get it right. Though I fall short of God's glory so many times, He always forgives me and reminds me that He loves me and that He will never leave me or forsake me. God, you are such a loving Father. Thank you, Daddy God, for without you my life would be meaningless.

To my Husband, William Brookins, you are such a patient man. God could not have given me a better partner to do life with. Thank you for staying. We have had our many ups and downs. There were moments when we were hit so hard, by the enemy, that we didn't think we were going to get back up. But God!! He always showed us our purpose in each other's eyes, and He gave us the will to fight to see what the end is going to be. For this, I love you. I once thought I knew what love was until I met you and God gave me a whole new meaning of true love. Thank you, baby.

To my children: Ejay, Kay, Zay, and Liv. Thank you for allowing mommy the time to write this book. Thank you for the many days you allowed the house to remain peaceful and quiet so I can get my work done. There were many days I would be in the home office writing, and I would hear one of you say, "Shhh, Mommy is writing her book." I smiled and chuckled to myself and said, "Lord thank you for my babies." I'm truly blessed to have you in my life, and I am honored that God chose me to be your mother. You are some AWESOME kids, and mommy loves you all so much!

To my Big Ma, Catherine Owens, thank you for being my lifeline. You saved me during a time that I didn't even know that I needed to be saved. Thank you for your guidance, your wisdom, and your love. I am honored to be your namesake and your granddaughter. I love you, pretty Lady!

To my mentor, Cyrene Wright M.D., thank you for always being a phone call away. Thank you for your many prayers and Bible study sessions. Thank you for always yielding to the Holy Spirit and giving me much needed godly counsel. I am forever grateful for the wisdom you poured into me.

To my Sister-in-love, Victoria James-Banks. Thank you for not only being my sister but being my friend. You believed in my vision when others doubted it. You have supported my vision and believed in me. You have trusted me, prayed for me, and you have encouraged me. Thank you for seeing my vision, taking my hand, and running with me. You are truly amazing. I love you, Sis!

To my editor, my publisher, and my inspiration, MP Sudduth. If you only knew how much you inspire me to do what I do. You are an amazing business woman. I have enjoyed watching you work from afar, and now I am honored to finally get the opportunity to work with you on my book project. You are kind and compassionate, and you get my vision. I love working with you. Thank you for taking the time out to help me perfect my purpose. You are truly a Godsend. Love ya girl!

Thank you to Beyond The Book Media, LLC and Chanel E. Martin. I could not have written my manuscript without your program. Who knew I could write a book in such a short amount of time. I thought it would take years, but you showed me that it could be done in weeks. You teach people how to partner with the Holy Spirit and let Him guide them through the writing process. I am forever grateful for the knowledge I received from your program. May God send many more people your way because your program, 21 Day Author Bootcamp, really works!

To my accountability group (Adrianna, Analesse, Bisi, and Juli), from Beyond the Book Media, thank you ladies for always checking in and holding me accountable to get my manuscript done. I really appreciate all of you.

Thank you to the many wives who will pick up my book and read it. Just know that it was only by God's design that this book caught your eye. I pray that this book gives you the strategies you need to keep pressing forward in your marriage. May God be the glue that holds you and your husband together, forever and always.

Thank you to my many family, friends, and church members who encouraged me along the way. You are my push.

REFERENCES

Bible Gateway. (1993). Access your bible from anywhere. BibleGateway.com: A searchable online Bible in over 150 versions and 50 languages. Retrieved from https://www.biblegateway.com/

Meyer, J. (1995). *Battlefield of the mind: Winning the battle in your mind*. Faith Words.

Tyndale House Publishers. (2015). Holy bible: New living translation.

YouVersion. (2008). Creating experiences to encourage & challenge people to seek God daily. YouVersion. Retrieved from https://www.youversion.com/

ABOUT THE AUTHOR

Katherine Brookins is native of Chicago, IL and the founder and CEO of Divine Motivation, LLC in Illinois. She holds a bachelor's degree in Political Science, and is currently pursuing a master's degree in Communication from Liberty University. She attends Rhema Word Kingdom Ministries in Riverdale, IL.

She enjoys praise dancing, reading, listening to music, and listening to a good preached word on YouTube. She often gives words of encouragement to listeners on her podcast, Divine Motivation for Wives and Mothers. Her desire is to see marriages and families healed, healthy, lasting, and thriving.

She and her husband, William, have been married for nearly 13 years and have a lifetime to go. They have a Facebook page called Marriage Surgery, where they encourage other married couples to keep pressing forward in their marriage. They have a blended family, and altogether, they have six beautiful children: three girls and three boys.

You can also find the author here:
www.marriagesurgery.com
www.divinemotivation4wm.com
https://www.facebook.com/groups/wivesonamissiontoendure

Manufactured by Amazon.ca
Bolton, ON

25400657R00058